CONTENTS

D0815065

MAP

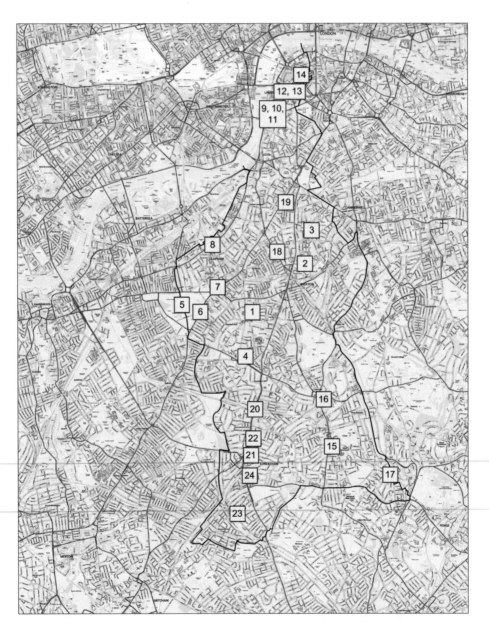

The London Borough of Lambeth

(Contains Ordnance Survey data © Crown copyright and database right 2012).

Key:

AROUND BRIXTON

(1) The Margate Road Horror

(2) 'Supernormal' Disturbances at The Gresham Arms

(3) The House that Haunted Roy Hudd

AROUND CLAPHAM

(4) The Devil in Disguise?

(5) Strange Tales from Clapham Common

(6) The Spectral Hansom Cab of South Side

(7) The Haunting of the Plough Inn

(8) The Black Dog of Wandsworth Road

AROUND NORTH LAMBETH

(9) Ghost Stories of Lambeth Palace

(10) The Tomb of the Tradescants

(11) Mercy Weller's Ghost

(12) The Predatory Lift of Lincoln House

(13) The Lingering Shadow of Waterloo's Necropolis Railway

(14) Ghosts at The Old Vic

AROUND NORWOOD

(15) The Ghost of Norwood

(16) Tulse Hill Station and the Phantom Footsteps of Platform One

(17) Gipsy Hill: Fortune Tellers and a Headless Phantom

AROUND STOCKWELL

(18) The Stockwell Ghost

(19) A Ghost on the Northern Line

AROUND STREATHAM

(20) The Many Ghosts of Caesars Nightclub

(21) The Haunted House of Shrubbery Road

(22) The Phantom of the Cinema

(23) A Mysterious Light in Tankerville Road

(24) The Phantom Nun of Coventry Hall

ACKNOWLEDGEMENTS

THIS book could not have been written without a great deal help from many people, including but not limited to: Lionel Beer (Travel and Earth Mysteries Society); John M. Clarke (author of *The Brookwood Necropolis Railway);* Jon Crampton (media relations officer, Network Rail); Rebecca Geary (Make Space Studios); Sally Hamlyn (marketing and publicity officer, Museum of Garden History – now the Garden Museum); Roy Hudd (www.royhudd. com); Darren Mann (www.paranormal-database.com); William McCormack; Sussannah Mortimer (cinema manager, Odeon Streatham); Philip Norman (volunteer curatorial assistant, Museum of Garden History – now the Garden Museum); Elizabeth Norton (author of *Anne Boleyn: In Her Own Words & the Words of Those Who Knew Her);* Andrew Nunn (premises and administration secretary to the Archbishop of Canterbury); Ann Osborn (head of the Junior Department, Fairley House School); Mustapha Ousellam; Alan Piper; Ned Seago (stage-door manager, The Old Vic); Dolly Sen (www.dollysen. com); Anne Ward (archivist, Lambeth Archives and Minet Library); and the following users of www.railforums. co.uk: 'Capybara', 'Clip', 'KiddyKid', 'SalopSparky', 'steamybrian', and 'thedbdiboy'. My sincere apologies to anyone I should have mentioned by name but overlooked.

Thanks also to Jayne Ayris for looking over the (almost) completed book and providing invaluable feedback; Anthony Wallis for the amazing illustrations he created (you can find him at www.ant-wallis-illustration.blogspot.co.uk); and my family for all of their support and encouragement. Finally, a special credit must go to my brother's IT company, www.prehocsolutions.co.uk, for rescuing my early work on this book after my PC suffered a catastrophic systems error.

INTRODUCTION

LAMBETH is an odd place. As an entity the borough is the sum of many contrasting parts, its borders cutting out a long, narrow cross-section through south London. From the busy tourist attractions beside the River Thames in the north, the borough encompasses very different areas of varying degrees of prosperity as it stretches south, through built-up districts and down towards relatively leafier suburbs.

The reason for this somewhat confused identity is that, as with London as a whole, the borough of Lambeth is an amalgamation of what were once separate villages surrounded by open countryside. To help make sense of this patchwork personality, the borough is often considered to comprise six general neighbourhoods: Brixton; Clapham; North Lambeth (including Waterloo, Kennington, Oval, and Vauxhall); Norwood (including West Norwood, Gipsy Hill, and Tulse Hill); Stockwell; and Streatham (including Streatham Hill and Streatham Vale). The present book has been organised along these lines.

Something these differing areas have in common with each other – as they do with the rest of the vast London

metropolis – is a rich heritage of strange stories, telling of apparitions, poltergeists, and all manner of other bizarre wonders. The tales described here were collected for Project Albion, an on-going programme by ASSAP (the Association for the Scientific Study of Anomalous Phenomena) to record and collate such mysteries and folklore from across the British Isles in what has been called a 'Domesday Book of the paranormal'. You can find out more about Project Albion and ASSAP at the association's website: www.assap.ac.uk.★

Are the tales recounted in the following pages true? Well, the stories are certainly real, in as much as they were reported in newspapers, written about in books, and/or circulated via all manner of other means, including simple word of mouth. To that extent, they give a glimpse of what might be called the mythological landscape of Lambeth, and if nothing else this offers an interesting perspective on places you might have thought you knew.

As for the objective reality or otherwise of the incidents related – well, that's something you'll have to decide for yourself! Whatever conclusions you reach, the journey involved in uncovering your neighbourhood's stranger side can be truly fascinating. Read on to discover the unnatural history of Haunted Lambeth ...

James Clark, 2013

* I have previously collected tales for Project Albion from the London Borough of Wandsworth (Lambeth's neighbour to the east) and from Mitcham in the London Borough of Merton; for further information about these, see my website at www.james-clark.co.uk.

1

AROUND BRIXTON

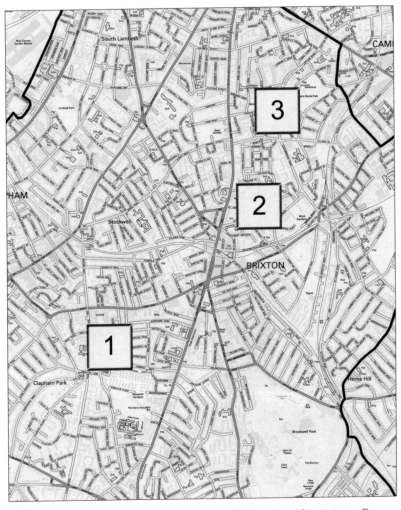

AROUND BRIXTON. *Key: (1) The Margate Road Horror; (2) 'Supernormal' Disturbances at The Gresham Arms; (3) The House that Haunted Roy Hudd. (Contains Ordnance Survey data © Crown copyright and database right 2012.)*

The Margate Road Horror

In July 1979, American cinema audiences were terrified by *The Amityville Horror*. The silver-screen version of a bestselling book by Jay Anson, it told the – purportedly true – story of an American family who fled their home in fear after being plagued by supernatural events. That same year a somewhat similar tale emerged from Brixton in south London.

Until around two years before, the Victorian house in Margate Road had been home to Randolph Galway, a clerk in his mid-forties, and his wife Stasia. They had been happily married for thirteen years but their marriage began to suffer soon after they moved into the house. According to newspaper reports, Randolph became depressed and turned to alcohol, sneering at his wife when she repeatedly claimed to have seen a 'strange ghostly form like a dog with horns'. After about six weeks, Stasia announced that she could not bear to stay in the house any longer. She left her husband, taking their two children with her.

Margate Road, the setting for a tale of supernatural horror in the 1970s.

The night after she left, Randolph let himself into the empty house and saw what he was convinced was a 'black goat' running down the stairs. The dark shape rushed past him and out through the front door – and it was at that moment, he later told reporters, that he 'decided the house was haunted'. He moved out, quit drinking, and his wife and children came back to him.

After the Galways left, the property was purchased by the council, who renovated and redecorated it. In late 1979, the house became home to thirty-three-year-old unemployed driver Peter Richardson, his wife Linda, and their five children. Once again, it took just six weeks for the occupants to be driven from the building.

During those 'six weeks of hell', as Peter later described them, hardly a day went by without some uncanny happening frightening the Richardsons. One night, a 'cold, smoky sort of shadow' hovered above the bed, touching Linda (who was pregnant at the time with their sixth child) on her arm. Another time, Linda and one of her daughters, aged twelve, watched a doll walk across the settee by itself. On a third occasion the family's youngest daughter, aged five, told her mother that she had seen her talking to another woman, though no one else was in the house at the time.

One night, around the beginning of December, it all became too much to bear. Peter had gone out for the evening, the children were in bed, and Linda was alone watching the television. Suddenly she saw a footstool move by itself from one side of the room to the other. 'I sat petrified, unable to move,' she later told the *News of the World*. 'Then the room went crazy. A china doll flew at me and smashed on the table in front of me. Birthday cards were flying around the room and things were falling over. By this time I'd gone to pieces. I screamed.'

When Peter returned home he found Linda so upset that they did not wait until dawn but simply took the children and fled, abandoning many of their possessions.

Afterwards, the house was visited by Henry 'Harry' Cleverley, an assistant district housing manager with Lambeth Council who also happened to be a trance medium. The moment Harry stepped over the threshold, he sensed a disturbing presence. He was unable to tell whether it was male or female but had no doubt at all that it was hostile. He ordered it to depart and was surprised when it seemed to obey him. However, a moment later, as he walked back into the middle of the room, the threatening presence returned.

Harry felt sure that Linda had psychic abilities she was unaware of, and that her sensitivity to spirits would make it impossible for her to live peacefully in this house. He promised to find the Richardsons somewhere else to live. The family moved into a nearby vacant property and the council agreed they could remain there as squatters until a new home was found for them.

'We have no plans to exorcise the ghost, or whatever it is,' declared a council spokesman, who stated that the house was to be re-let as soon as possible.

Harry Cleverley, however, decided to deal with the problem himself in his capacity as a medium. Some three weeks later he returned to the house accompanied by a team of spiritualists. Also present was journalist Diana Hutchinson, who reported on the visit for the *Daily Mail*. When the group entered the house, they saw open drawers and abandoned clothes, an unnerving reminder of the family who had fled these rooms in panic not so long before.

The plan, Harry told the journalist, was to exorcise any spirits present in the building, although he was scathing of the Church of England's approach to exorcism. According to him, that was nothing more than 'ritual mumbo jumbo' and it was simply not possible to dispel spirits by 'sprinkling water and mouthing prayers'. He explained that he would go into a trance and invite any spirits present to speak through him. Another medium, Peggy Holmes, was to act as 'interpreter' between the spirits and the group, while Peggy's husband, Ray, and another team member, Angela Palmer, would protect Harry by acting as 'friendly power-houses'.

The intrepid group crowded into the small bedroom at the front of the house. Harry entered a trance and very quickly began screaming, growling, and swearing. Peggy spoke to him in reassuring, level tones, asking the spirit that was apparently manifesting through him to talk about his or her (or its) problems, but this only seemed to make the spirit angrier. Harry began to flail his arms around wildly, screaming in fury as he bounced around the bed.

Eventually, the hullabaloo subsided. Still in trance, Harry continued to mutter darkly as Peggy spoke to him in a soothing, sing-song voice. She encouraged the spirit(s) to depart, to look towards the light where friends were waiting to help, and after about an hour she announced: 'It's over. I think they've gone away.'

The Richardson family had previously suggested that the strange happenings were connected to the suicide of a woman some years before. They had heard she had hanged herself in the house after her husband died (although the police stated that they had no record of this). The spiritualists, however, came up with a different answer.

Through Harry's mediumship, they found that the spirits troubling the house were those of a man and woman who had lived there at some point in the property's history and who might have dabbled in black magic. They were 'full of hatred and violence', claimed the spiritualists, and they resented anyone else living in what they clearly felt was still their home.

But that was all in the past now. Harry was confident that the exorcism had been a success and that the house would in future be unaffected by supernatural turmoil.

Despite such reassurances, however, the Richardson family were resolute that nothing would ever persuade them to move back into that house in Margate Road.

'Supernormal' Disturbances at The Gresham Arms

Strange goings-on in Brixton at the beginning of the twentieth century were 'undoubtedly the work of some supernormal agency'. Such was the opinion of an author writing in the spiritualist journal *Light* in September 1900. This author, whose name was given only as W.C.L., reported that bells at The Gresham Arms pub in Fyfield Road had been 'ringing separately and collectively, at all hours of the night and day, for the last five months.'

Furthermore, inexplicable footsteps were heard on the stairs from time to time, and doors would bang during the night. A second writer – *see* below – added that 'other occurrences of a mysterious nature – such as the lighting of gas after a room had been closed and locked for the night – often took place.'

The pub's proprietor (a gentleman named Mr Welch), along with the manageress, the potman (a soldier recently returned from the front), and the barmaid all attested to the fact that these events had been taking place, and W.C.L. himself (or herself) confirmed that he (or she) had 'seen and heard every bell on the premises ring at midday!' Two barmaids had apparently quit as a result of these disturbances.

Mr Welch considered himself a sceptic with regard to the supernatural, but was a practical man interested only in getting rid of the nuisance as quickly as possible. To that end he gave permission for a seance to be held on the premises, and this duly took place on Tuesday, 11 September 1900.

The medium involved was a lady named Mrs Brenchley, who was reportedly unfamiliar with either the pub or the area in general. Her psychic sensitivities suggested to her that the happenings were linked to a death in the house, and according to W.C.L. a man had indeed dropped down dead in the bar a few months before. Perhaps significantly, the unfortunate man in question had apparently been singing 'Those bells shall not ring out' just before he died.

The medium walked from room to room, and the others taking part in the seance followed her, listening as she gave her impressions of various other deaths she felt were connected with the building's history.

At one point, she indicated a particular window and claimed that a coffin had been lowered through it (a detail that W.C.L. reported was subsequently verified).

However, despite Mrs Brenchley's abilities the seance failed to establish a precise reason for the apparent haunting. Neither did it succeed in putting a stop to the disturbances.

A few months later a second writer, Thomas Atwood, wrote a description of another investigation at the building. Once again, this was published in *Light*. As with the seance described above,

This attractively restored building was once The Gresham Arms pub.

Atwood's investigation was carried out during the autumn of 1900, but this time the participants consisted of a committee of seven unnamed gentlemen.

They were given permission to hold seances in one of the building's rooms and, under Atwood's direction, they held a series of sittings over the course of several weeks. They intended to encourage the spirits they believed were attached to the premises to communicate with them, although all agreed that it would be dangerous for any of the sitters to enter a full trance and allow a spirit to take control of him. From Atwood's subsequent report, it seems that this was a wise precaution:

> At our first sitting the presence of a powerful spirit, clairvoyantly seen, and described as repulsive in the extreme, was sensed by all sitters. He made several attempts to entrance one of the sitters, which, by a strongly combined effort, were successfully resisted. The impression left on the minds of most, if not all, of the sitters was that if this spirit had once got control, it would have been a case of what may best be described in three words: 'hell let loose'.

Fortunately, apart from some shaken nerves, none of the sitters suffered any harm, and during the committee's subsequent sittings they believed that they made contact with 'many poor spirits', which they were able to help. However, none of the spirits they contacted seemed in any way to be connected with the happenings at the pub.

Despite the committee's best efforts, wrote Atwood, their attempt to 'arrive at the truth as regards the alleged manifestations … concluded without a scrap of evidence of their existence … although, in fairness, it should be stated that one of our number declared that he personally had witnessed the ringing of the bells under circumstances that, in his opinion, precluded any suspicion of fraud.'

Nevertheless, Atwood stated that as soon as his group began their first sitting all the phenomena at The Gresham Arms ceased, so the proprietor, if no one else, must have been pleased at the outcome.

The Gresham Arms no longer exists. The shell of the old building has been attractively restored, and it now houses a number of apartments.

The House that Haunted Roy Hudd

Born in Croydon on 16 May 1936, the actor and comedian Roy Hudd is acknowledged as an authority on the history of music hall. His love for that bygone era of entertainment is genuine and infectious, but the story of how he first became familiar with one of music hall's greatest stars makes for a very strange tale indeed.

In Richard Davis's 1979 book *I've Seen a Ghost! True Stories from Show Business*, Roy told how, for as long as he could remember, he had dreamed the same recurring dream. Finding himself outside a house that had a porch with a stone pillar to either side, he would walk up a short flight of stone steps to the front door, push it open and walk inside, into a hall. Sometimes he would enter the room to his right – a fairly small room – and at other times he would walk into the room to his left.

It was the latter room he found most interesting. It ran all the way from the front of the house to the back, and it featured an unusual round sofa in the centre. At the far end a door led to a flight of steps, which in turn led down to the garden. Roy only ever 'saw' this garden at night, and whenever he did it was hung with decorative fairy lights.

The dream would always end the same way, with Roy in the cellar, seemingly surrounded by numerous other versions of him all standing in the same pose. As the years passed he came to understand this as meaning that the cellar walls were lined with mirrors.

One day, in around 1962 or 1963, Roy received an invitation from two actor friends of his to visit them at their new flat. The address they gave was in Akerman Road, Brixton, not too far away from Roy's own home, and so he and his wife Ann got into their car and drove to see their friends.

Roy was unfamiliar with Brixton – yet, as they turned the corner into Akerman Road, he had the disturbing feeling that he had been there before. The couple drove slowly along the road, looking for the address they had been given, and as they passed one particular house, Roy suddenly announced: 'This is it, this is the house!'

His wife told him not to be silly. They had never been there before and could see no number on the door. But Roy stubbornly insisted that this was the correct house, saying that he recognised the porch. As soon as the car stopped he leapt out and hurried up the stone steps to the front door, increasingly certain that he knew this building.

Ann joined him and rang the bell – and must have been surprised when the people who answered did indeed turn out to be their friends. She was even more surprised when her husband pushed his way past them without even saying hello, muttering, 'I know this house' as he entered the hall.

As his nonplussed friends looked on, Roy indicated the room to the right and described the interior to them, before looking inside and confirming that the room was indeed just as it appeared in his dreams. He then described the room to his left.

'It was just how I'd always seen it,' he recalled afterwards. 'There was no round sofa, but the staircase leading down to the garden was there.'

He sat down, 'white-faced and shaking', before turning to his 'completely bewildered' companions and telling them about his recurring dream. After a long pause, they explained why they had been so keen for him to see their new home. They told Roy that between 1898 and 1901 the house had been home to a famous Victorian music-hall comedian named Dan Leno, and they took Roy outside to show him the commemorative plaque hanging on the wall.

It was the first time Roy had ever heard of Dan Leno, but from that day on he was determined to learn as much about him as he could.

Born George Galvin in December 1860, the son of a show-business family, Dan Leno found early fame as a clog dancer and went on to become a great pantomime performer and the most popular comedian of his day. Sadly, the strain of continuous performance proved too much and, at the height of his popularity, Leno suffered a nervous breakdown. He died, aged just

Roy Hudd's 'dream house' in Akerman Road. The blue plaque on the wall reads: 'Dan Leno (1860–1904), Music-hall comedian, lived here, 1898–1901'.

forty-three, on 31 October 1904, physically and mentally exhausted.

Roy's interest in Dan Leno led to him presenting the preface to a televised version of Leno's autobiography, in which Roy told viewers the story of his recurring dream. Afterwards, he started to receive numerous letters – from Leno fans, Brixton residents, spiritualists, mediums, and ex-music hall performers. Without exception, the letters were what Roy described as 'good, happy and optimistic'.

The fans and Brixton residents 'all extolled [Leno's] virtues,' Roy stated. 'He was obviously greatly loved and loving.' The spiritualists and mediums wanted Roy to know that Leno 'was forever "getting in touch" with cheerful messages', and many of the performers claimed that Leno's ghost had appeared to them at the Theatre Royal, Drury Lane, in London's West End. (For more about the ghosts said to haunt the Theatre Royal, see my 2007 book *Haunted London*.)

Everyone seemed to believe that Leno would be a helpful influence on Roy's life.

Acknowledged as an authority on the history of music-hall entertainment, Roy Hudd's first acquaintance with one of its greatest stars came about in a very strange way. (Photograph courtesy of Roy Hudd Enterprises: www.royhudd.com)

As one thespian letter writer put it: 'He's keeping a paternal eye on a fellow toiler in the greasepaint vineyard.'

Another similarity between the letter writers was that nearly everyone warned Roy that he should never visit Leno's grave. Roy recalled: 'I must admit I had a shiver over these when I discovered I was living barely a mile from where he was buried [in Lambeth Cemetery, south London]. Of course I "poo-poohed" the whole idea in public but I never did visit his grave. Well, you never know, do you?'

As Roy learned about Dan Leno's life he discovered details that seemed to explain elements of his dream. Because Leno had been a dancer he used to practice in front of mirrors, and this led Roy to wonder if the walls of the cellar in Akerman Road had once been hung with mirrors. If so, then perhaps this might explain the multiple images of himself that he had dreamed about so many times. He also learned that Leno had held parties at the Brixton house, for which he would have the garden hung with fairy lights – just as Roy had seen so often in his dream.

He would never see those lights again, though. In October 2011 Roy Hudd confirmed to me that, from the moment he visited Akerman Road, he ceased to dream about the house, and never dreamt of it again.

2

AROUND CLAPHAM

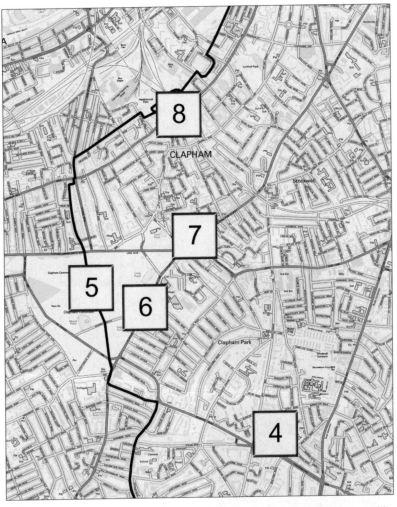

AROUND CLAPHAM. *Key: (4) The Devil in Disguise?; (5) Strange Tales from Clapham Common; (6) The Spectral Hansom Cab of South Side; (7) The Haunting of the Plough Inn; (8) The Black Dog of Wandsworth Road. (Contains Ordnance Survey data © Crown copyright and database right 2012.)*

The Devil in Disguise?

In 1994, the *South London Press* newspaper carried a bizarre story. According to the reports, a council flat was being haunted by a 'demon' – one that appeared in the guise of Elvis Presley! Presley died in 1977.

The flat in question was located in Pearce House on the Clapham Park Estate in Tilson Gardens. It was home to Shirley, aged thirty-one, a fan of the late singer. The first person to experience anything odd there was Shirley's friend Josie of nearby Tilson House. At about 1.30 p.m. on 9 February 1994, Shirley and Josie were sitting in the flat, drinking tea and watching television. Josie later said:

> Shirley gave me a pack of cards of Elvis to hold … While I sat here, I started shaking and saw what I thought was Elvis just standing across the sitting room – I started screaming and crying,

Pearce House, where frightening events were reported in 1994.

I don't know why. It was just standing there, about 5ft 7in tall. I couldn't see its eyes. Then it just changed into a white figure. It all lasted for about two minutes.

Shirley did not see what her friend saw, but following the incident she began to worry that her three-year-old son had started talking to an invisible man in the flat. It seemed to her that the unseen entity was attempting to lure the young boy to the second-floor flat's window ledge, and she was scared he would fall or jump out.

Later, Shirley was herself confronted by the terrifying vision of a 'five-month-old foetus' hovering in the kitchen.

The frightening events sent her to her local vicar for help, and on 15 February the Revd Chris Ivory of Christ Church, Christchurch Road, came round to bless the flat. Despite his efforts, Shirley continued to experience eerie occurrences after the blessing, including seeing black smoke in the sitting room.

In desperation, she applied to Lambeth Council for a transfer to a different flat. She did not mention the strange happenings on her application form. The council placed her on a transfer list but did not consider her case to be a priority.

Stuck where she was for the time being, Shirley asked more churchmen and a medium to visit the flat to get rid of the unwanted entity. The outcome of the medium's visit was not reported in the newspaper but on 4 March the flat was once again blessed, this time by the Revd Noel Cooper of All Saints' church, Lyham Road, Clapham Park, accompanied by a former parishioner named Bert. They said prayers with Shirley to strengthen her against any repeat of the disturbing incidents. Following their visit, things seem to settle down.

Strange Tales from Clapham Common

Many stories in folklore involve spaces that could be described as 'liminal', meaning that they lie at the boundary between different places or states. The intersection of ways at a crossroads, for example, can be thought of as a liminal zone; other examples might include bridges and rivers. Perhaps Clapham Common could be considered as something of a liminal place, in that, as well as being an area of greenery in the midst of an otherwise urban landscape, it straddles the border of Lambeth and Wandsworth boroughs. From this boundary region have emerged many strange tales.

The Whistling Stone

Elliot O'Donnell, that prolific (if less than reliable) teller of colourful ghost stories, wrote in his *More Haunted Houses of London* (1920) of Clapham Common's 'Whistling Stone'. Apparently, this large white stone had once stood in a hollow on the common but it had gone by the time he searched for it in the autumn of 1900.

Although O'Donnell never personally heard the stone whistle, he wrote that several people told him they had. One was an old vagrant who, whilst wandering across the common one foggy night in search of a suitable place to sleep, had suddenly heard someone whistling 'a very plaintive air'. Because the late hour and inclement weather would have kept most folk indoors, he presumed it must be another vagrant and set off to find him or her.

As he walked, the sound grew louder. He knew therefore that he was heading in the right direction, but he became puzzled when, at the place where the sound was loudest, he could see no one. There was nothing there, in fact, save for a large white stone. Leaning closer, he was shocked to discover that the stone itself was the source of the alluring sound. Thereafter, whenever he walked across the common he always visited the stone in the hope of once again hearing the beautiful music.

O'Donnell recounts a second story from a vagrant, this one from an old woman known as 'blue-necked Sally' on account of a bluish-coloured scar on her neck. Sally told him that one night, as she lay sleeping on the common, she was awoken by a sweetly whistled melody so full of melancholic beauty that it made her weep. Near where she had been lying was a stone, and when Sally bent close and pressed her ear to it it became clear that this was where the sad music was coming from. The whistling continued for a few minutes before it ceased, but it returned the following night at around the same time.

In an attempt to find some explanation for this curious phenomenon, O'Donnell made many inquiries and was told two tales which he recorded, although he said he doubted the trustworthiness of either of them. One story was that the stone stood on the spot where an old peddler had been murdered. The other was that 'an old crossing sweeper, who used to sell whistles, made from the branches of the trees on the Common' had once been discovered there, frozen to death.

The bandstand on Clapham Common.

The Devil's Skittle Alley

During the late nineteenth century, perhaps while the 'Whistling Stone' still stood in its hollow, visitors to Clapham Common might have also stumbled across a striking configuration of nine elm trees. The author of 'A Few Recollections of Clapham: The Common During the Past Sixty Years' (*Clapham Observer*, 1 February 1924) wrote that these elms were arranged 'as the nine skittles are on a skittle-board' and stood near to where the bandstand was later built. A large protuberance at the base of one of the elms was shaped 'somewhat like a skittle-ball', while a short distance away, in direct line with the elms, stood a pair of poplar trees.

According to this author, the poplars 'were supposed to represent His Satanic Majesty and a man engaged in a game of skittles' and the area was popularly known as the 'Devil's Skittle Alley'.

A Journey through Time

From the twentieth century comes a curious account of time seemingly going awry for one man on Clapham Common. Although almost certainly a tall tale, it's a great yarn and one well worth repeating here. It was recorded by John Bradbury in a three-part article that appeared in the *South Western Star* in 1982 and, as near as I have been able to ascertain, the events described supposedly occurred in the late 1960s.

Freddie Snucher (or Snusher) was an old man then but in his youth he had worked on the fairgrounds with the gypsies and earned money fighting in the boxing booths around Mitcham. It had been a hard life, and one that had toughened him considerably. His face was tanned and leathered from the many years spent outdoors, and despite the arthritis in his hands he was always ready to lift a pint or two of bitter at his favourite pub, the Windmill at Clapham Common – especially if someone else offered to pay.

A superstitious man, Freddie always carried a battered old pack of Tarot cards around with him and, if you caught him in the right mood, he would happily tell you your future. One evening, Freddie was persuaded to deal the cards to himself. It soon became clear to the regulars gathered around that the reading was far from good. With every card he looked at, Freddie seemed to grow more fearful. All at once he swept the cards into his pocket, downed the remains of his whisky, and strode towards the exit. In the doorway he paused for a moment to mutter what the bemused onlookers heard as 'Bloody Loon!' and then he was gone, the door swinging closed behind him.

Afterwards, Freddie would claim that he knew something terrible was going to happen to him because he had dealt to himself 'the most scary card of the whole deck': the moon, representing hidden dangers, enemies and threats. The French name for this card is 'La Lune' and this is what he had actually cursed as he left the pub: 'Bloody Lune!'

A few days later, news came to the regulars that Freddie had been taken to St James's Hospital in Balham. He had been found unconscious the night before at the foot of an elm tree on Clapham Common, having suffered a heart attack. Fortunately, he recovered, and when he did so he gave a truly fantastical account of what had happened to him.

After enjoying two pints of bitter at a pub (not the Windmill), he had been making his way home. Having walked up Battersea Rise, he was already about halfway there, striding across the common in the direction of his small one-room flat in Elms Road. The light was beginning to fade and ahead of him, in the misty gloom on the other side of the bandstand, he thought for a moment that he glimpsed an old-fashioned windmill. Of course, he knew it was nothing but a trick of the light, an illusion born of swirling mist and the gathering darkness and, sure enough, as he drew nearer the image disappeared.

The Windmill on the Common pub.

Yet something remained off-kilter. Visually, nothing appeared out of place, but there was something 'not quite right' about the smell of the common: it felt somehow more rural than usual. The sounds too were just a little bit wrong and the combination provoked a gnawing sense of unease.

Freddie hurried past the children's playground, eager to reach the bright lights of the road and see other people, yet the road seemed to get no nearer. A distant voice called out an echoing name, 'Tom-Tom Crenshaw-caw-caw', disturbing a nearby group of crows who answered with harsh croaks as they took to the air and flew away over the Mount Pond.

There was still no sign of the road as Freddie reached a deeply rutted cart track that he had never seen before. By now quite unnerved, he turned to run, desperate to retrace his route and return to familiar surroundings. As he did so, his foot caught against something hard, sending him sprawling into the grass. When he looked up he saw that the mysterious windmill had reappeared.

It loomed above him, its canvas sails creaking as they turned. A steep flight of steps led up to a door into the mill itself. Beside him, perfectly solid, was the wooden beam that had tripped him. He saw now that this was the windmill's tail pole (the pole used to turn the main body so that the sails faced into the wind).

There could be no doubt that the old-fashioned windmill was real and yet Freddie knew perfectly well that no windmill existed there, at least not anymore, and as he struggled to make sense of his situation the only conclusion his panicked mind could reach was that he had somehow travelled back in time. He was, he believed, trapped within a

Mound Pond, Clapham Common.

'time bubble'. To make matters worse, he could catch tantalising glimpses of his own, twentieth-century reality through the bubble's walls. Yet no matter how much he struggled, punching and kicking wildly in his efforts to escape, the windmill persisted. At last, exhausted and with his heart thumping, he took hold of the stair rail to steady himself.

Then he spotted a motionless figure at the mill door, silhouetted against the moon. As Freddie watched, the figure seemed to mimic his movements: as he wiped the sweat from his forehead the figure did the same, and when Freddie reached into his coat pocket to feel the comforting familiarity of his front-door keys, the shadowy figure produced a key of its own and with it opened the door to the windmill. Then it turned to Freddie, and beckoned to him to come closer.

Confusion, terror, and the strain of his exertions had taken Freddie to the brink of his sanity and, with one last despairing thought, he decided to take the initiative and confront the figure. He seized the handrail and charged up the stairs. At that moment, reality shifted again.

Abruptly, the 'time bubble' seemed to retreat, first the windmill and then the surrounding landscape becoming smaller as the bubble lifted and soared away towards the moon. Freddie found himself falling. Desperately, he reached out towards the figure but it disintegrated into dead leaves. He fell to the ground and blacked out. Passers-by found him some time later, lying unconscious at the base of an elm tree, and he was taken to hospital.

Freddie claimed to believe he had travelled back in time, and it is true that a windmill that could match his description once stood on the common. It was a post-mill, probably built in the late fourteenth century, which in the mid-seventeenth century was leased to one Thomas Crenshaw. According to tradition, this windmill burned down in the autumn of 1666 (the year of the Great Fire of London, although this incident was unrelated to that conflagration) and Crenshaw was killed trying to put the flames out.

As stated earlier, though, Freddie's adventure was almost certainly a tall tale invented by him for his own amusement and the entertainment of anyone who cared to listen. Bradbury admitted as much when he wrote his account, and felt sure that he must have previously mentioned the old windmill to Freddie. Even if he had not, considering that Freddie drank in a pub called the Windmill in a road on the edge of the common called Windmill Drive, he could probably have guessed that a windmill had at one time stood hereabouts! Yet, tall tale or not, there was apparently an interesting epilogue to the story.

Several weeks after being discovered unconscious on the common, Freddie's neighbours found him dead on his doorstep. There was nothing suspicious about the circumstances but Freddie's grown-up son, a flight sergeant in the RAF, later told Bradbury that the neighbours had found a key clutched in the dead man's hand. It was not, as might have been expected, the key to his front door but rather a key that appeared to be at least a couple of hundred years old …

UFOs

Even in the twenty-first century, Clapham Common continues to attract odd claims. A UFO is an Unidentified Flying Object; that is, any aerial object that the observer is unable to recognise. Whether or not any UFOs are, as some believe, extra-terrestrial spacecraft is another matter altogether, but if you want to try to find out then Clapham Common may be a good place to visit.

In April 2004, a tongue-in-cheek list of the UK's top 40 UFO 'hotspots' was published as part of an advertising campaign for Grolsch beer. Compiled by Nick Pope, who between 1991 and 1994 investigated UFO sightings on behalf of the Ministry of Defence, the list placed Clapham Common at number thirty-nine, just ahead of nearby Streatham.

The Spectral Hansom Cab of South Side

Invented in the late 1830s, the two-wheeled hansom cab was a great favourite with passengers. It was designed so that the driver sat on the outside at the back, giving the passengers a clear view of the route ahead. Time marches on and hansom cabs have long disappeared from our roads, but perhaps,

if you are especially lucky, you might just catch sight of a *spectral* hansom cab in the vicinity of Clapham Common.

In around 1900, Harry Smith Bilbe was a young man and a very keen cyclist. He often went for long rides and would not return home until the early hours of the morning. One summer morning at about 2 a.m., Harry was cycling home along Clapham Common South Side, enjoying the pleasantly empty moonlit road that stretched ahead of him, leading towards the cab rank in front of what was then the Plough Inn. (*See* 'The Haunting of the Plough Inn' for a separate ghost story from this establishment.)

'Suddenly,' wrote Harry in an account published in 1935:

> … from my near side and about a hundred yards ahead, there appeared a hansom cab. It came towards me on the tramlines, between which I was riding at about 17 miles an hour. My lamp was burning well, so I kept on, expecting the hansom to swing over to its near side – but it didn't. I swung to my near side, and looked up as I passed, intending to say something forcible to the driver, but was astonished to see that the driver's seat was *empty*!

As Harry slowed and watched, the hansom moved over to its near side and carried on past him, heading south-west towards Balham. Only then did Harry realise another peculiar feature about the cab. There was no rattling, no creaking, no clattering of hooves: in fact, there was absolutely no sound at all.

'Rubber tyres and hoof-pads,' he told himself in an attempt to rationalise the incident. Yet the encounter had clearly shaken him because, when he reached

Above: *Clapham Common South Side, looking in the direction of Balham. Was this road once haunted by a spectral hansom cab?*

Left: *Clapham South Underground station.*

the Plough, he pulled over and asked the man looking after a coffee stall there if he had seen the hansom.

'What 'ansom?' the man asked in reply.

When Harry explained that one had passed by just moments before, he received a disturbing response.

'That wasn't an' ansom, guv'nor.'

'What was it, then?'

'Dunno – but you ain't the first as says he's seen it on the common.'

Harry never found an explanation for what had happened that morning but it was not to be his only encounter with

that strange hansom cab. In the summer of 1934 he was once again travelling home, this time by car. With him were his wife – to whom he had previously told his bizarre story – and his two sons. The family had stayed out late visiting relatives in Clapham and it was about 12.30 a.m. as their car turned left out of Elms Road and onto South Side, heading towards Balham. The car's headlights were on and, as before, Harry had a clear view of the road ahead of him.

'I had barely "straightened up" when a hansom cab came across from the off-side, and travelled just ahead of me. My eldest boy, who sat with me in front, exclaimed: "Look, dad! What's that?" (He had never seen a hansom cab, except in pictures.)'

'That's your ghost cab, Harry … Take care!' exclaimed his wife.

The cab was travelling in the same direction as it had so many years earlier, but this time Harry was following it and he was determined to find out more. Ignoring his wife's warning, he declared: 'I'm going after it this time!' He accelerated but the cab abruptly swung over in front of his car, and just before they reached Clapham South Underground station the cab 'seemed to swing to the left – and was gone.' One moment it was dead ahead, in full view of Harry and his family; the next, the road was empty.

At least on this occasion Harry had witnesses to back up his uncanny experience: his wife and both sons had all seen the vehicle. However, the others were unfamiliar with the fact that the driver of a hansom sits perched up behind the cab, and so they did not notice what Harry did – that the driver's seat on this mysterious vehicle was once again completely empty.

The Haunting of the Plough Inn

With its gleaming white walls, black beams, and tall red-brick chimneys, the mock-Tudor exterior of the old building at 196 Clapham High Street evokes a reasonably convincing sense of the timeless English inn. A few years ago it was converted into an O'Neill's pub, but in a previous life it was known as the Plough. The name spoke of long-gone days when, as Walter Thornbury wrote in the 1870s, 'the village of Clapham, far removed from the busy hum of London life, was surrounded by green fields and homesteads'.

There has long been a pub or inn on this site: the present building was already about 150 years old in 1970, when new landlord Felwyn Williams and his wife moved in to what they soon discovered to be a strange new home. There had been reports of a spectre, known as 'Sarah', haunting the top two floors of the Plough since long before their arrival. A barman who lived on the premises had once awoken in the middle of the night to see the apparition of a white-clad woman standing by the bedroom window. The window was open and a strong breeze was blowing the curtains into the room, yet the woman's long black hair remained unruffled as she stood, silently, staring into space. Terrified, the barman leapt from his bed

The old Plough Inn (converted into an O'Neill's pub), photographed in 2012.

and rushed to awaken the landlord to tell him what he had seen. The next day the barman left, unwilling to remain a single night more.

Soon after Mr and Mrs Williams arrived, reports appeared in the local press of strange happenings on the upper floors of the Plough. Odd noises at night were making the resident staff uncomfortable and more than one member of staff believed they could feel the presence of 'Sarah' from time to time. As well as Mr and Mrs Williams, a further six members of staff resided in the pub. They were soon so nervous that, when it came time to retire to their rooms for the night, they would only venture upstairs in pairs.

In an article in the *South London Press* on 18 September 1970, Mr Williams was quoted as saying:

> There is definitely something ghostly in the pub. I have only been here eight weeks but I have found there are three rooms on the first floor where I get a very strange feeling. There is a musty smell and my hair stands on end. I get a prickly feeling in the corridor outside the rooms and so do several of my staff.

Mr Williams's dog, Rex, also seemed to sense something uncanny. He appeared frightened of certain rooms on the top floor and would not stray far from his master's or mistress' side.

Before coming to the Plough, Mr Williams had had no interest in ghosts, but now that he found himself living in an apparently haunted building he determined to do some investigation. He and the staff came to believe that the haunting had something to do with the tale of a barmaid who had been murdered in the inn sometime around the beginning of the twentieth century.

Eager to learn more, they decided to conduct seances in those rooms that seemed to be the most haunted. This they did by means of a makeshift Ouija board, laying out cards bearing letters and numbers on a table and selecting one card at a time by moving a glass. During one such seance, held in a disused room on the top floor, the glass spelled out the name 'Sarah' and a date, 'September 11'. This was only a day or so away, and as the date drew closer they all waited nervously to see what would happen.

On the designated night, the six resident staff returned to the top-floor room to keep vigil, but if they had hoped to witness the ghost of the murdered barmaid manifest itself they were disappointed. The night passed without incident.

Another strand to the story of a haunting at the Plough was the apparent mystery concerning the exact number of rooms on the top floor. Looking at the building from the outside, three windows were (and are) clearly visible on this floor, yet from the inside it appeared there should be only two. In some accounts of the haunting here it is claimed that the puzzling third window was sometimes seen from the outside to be open and at other times to be shut. The missing third window was eventually located in September 1970 when a hidden room was discovered, the doorway to which had been bricked up years before.

Writing in the *South Western Star* newspaper on 13 August 1982, John Bradbury stated that when the Plough had been given its mock-Tudor 'face-lift' in 1927 the 'two original windows were made to appear as three, to conform with Tudor style'. Before this date, he asserted, there had been only two windows on the top floor.

For Mr Williams, his efforts to find out more about the Plough's ghost had an unfortunate consequence. The inn's owners decided that the publicity was bad for business; they declared that everything had been the result of overactive imaginations, and removed Mr Williams from his post. In his book, *The Haunted Pub Guide*, Guy Lyon Playfair quite reasonably wonders why the owners made such a fuss. Publicity of this nature does not usually harm pubs at all – quite the opposite, in fact – and moreover none of the reported phenomena had been particularly sensational. It does appear as if the owners over-reacted to the situation.

Whether it was indeed all down to overactive imaginations, or whether the owners' actions had simply suppressed further talk of the ghost, by the time Andrew Green wrote about the Plough in his 1973 book *Our Haunted Kingdom* the tenancy had been taken over by a Mr Lynch, who informed Green that he had experienced no sign of the supernatural presence that had caused such trouble for Mr Williams.

Memory of those events seems to have faded over the years. In July 2008, William McCormack (manager of the new O'Neill's) told me that neither he nor any of his staff – 'all too young to remember the '70s' – had been aware of the story of 'Sarah' before I asked him.

Perhaps some lingering trace of her presence did remain, however, for Mr McCormack went on to mention that 'a lot of people that work here remark from time to time that there is an eerie feel about the place, especially late at night.'

The Black Dog of Wandsworth Road

Spectral black dogs are associated with many places in the British Isles. East Anglia, for example, has traditions of Old (or Black) Shuck; Yorkshire has the Barghest or Padfoot, the Isle of Man has the Moddhey (or Mauthe) Dhoo, and so on. For several weeks in 1962, Lambeth borough had its own spectral hound. It would appear at a fish restaurant in Wandsworth Road, just east of where the railway bridge from Wandsworth Road train station crosses above the traffic.

The restaurant had opened in April that year and, to begin with, business was great. But then a 'large, black and beautiful dog' mysteriously started to appear on the premises. On each occasion it was witnessed by three people (these seem to have been the owner, his wife, and a member of staff), and it always visited between 6 p.m. and 6.30 p.m. while the witnesses were sitting at a table in the empty restaurant.

Despite the back door of the building being locked, the dog would walk out from the rooms at the rear, pad through the restaurant, and step out of the front door into Wandsworth Road, where it would turn right and 'lope away up the main road and out of sight'.

If it were a ghost then it was a substantial one, because on one occasion it brushed against the wife's leg as it walked past and she reported that it felt quite solid.

The dog appeared on six or seven separate occasions over a period of six or seven weeks that summer. Following what turned out to be its final appearance, the restaurant's takings began to dip dramatically. The worried owner

Wandsworth Road. The phantom dog was reported to walk out of a restaurant that stood on the left, a little in front of the bridge, and 'lope away up the main road' (in the direction of the photographer).

wondered if the business's decline was somehow related to what he called the 'visitations' and this prompted him to write in December 1962 to the Society for Psychical Research. (The quotations above come from his letter to that august body.)

Investigation revealed a possible source for the canine phantom: it seems that a black dog belonging to a former owner of the restaurant had been run over and killed at a nearby crossroads, and all involved apparently concluded that the mysterious visitor had been the ghost of that dog.

The tale has a happy ending. Following a visit to the premises from a representative of the Society for Psychical Research, the owner reported that the restaurant was once again enjoying good business.

3

AROUND
NORTH LAMBETH

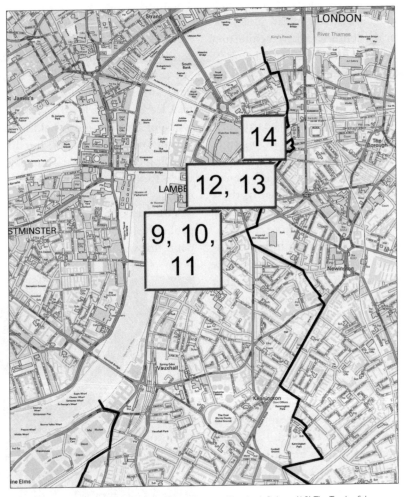

AROUND NORTH LAMBETH. *Key: (9) Ghost Stories of Lambeth Palace; (10) The Tomb of the Tradescants; (11) Mercy Weller's Ghost; (12) The Predatory Lift of Lincoln House; (13) The Lingering Shadow of Waterloo's Necropolis Railway; (14) Ghosts at The Old Vic. (Contains Ordnance Survey data © Crown copyright and database right 2012.)*

Ghost Stories of Lambeth Palace

Lambeth Palace has been a residence of the archbishops of Canterbury since the thirteenth century. Standing on the south bank of the Thames, at what was an ideal location to travel by boat across to Westminster, the palace was described by Walter Thornbury in the 1870s as a building that 'frowns down with mediaeval and almost feudal grandeur upon the waters of the river'. It certainly has an imposingly solemn air.

Over the centuries, many architectural changes have been made to Lambeth Palace and the oldest part of the building to survive today is the vaulted crypt or 'undercroft' that is now in use as a chapel. People have supposedly heard eerie sounds in this vicinity, sounds described as 'moaning and groaning' and 'the ghostly pleading of a woman's voice'. Although clear to begin with, these unsettling sounds are said to fade away if the hearer stops to listen more closely.

The sounds have been linked to the tragic tale of Queen Anne Boleyn, the second wife of King Henry VIII. After Anne failed to provide Henry with the son and heir he so desperately wanted, the king had her charged (almost certainly falsely) with adultery, incest with her brother, and high treason. According to one ghostly tradition, Anne's trial – conducted by Thomas Cranmer, the then Archbishop of Canterbury – was held in the crypt of Lambeth Palace, and the phantom sounds heard here are a supernatural echo of her weeping as she protests her innocence.

Another story claims that Anne's ghost has been seen at the riverside beside Lambeth Palace. Her apparition supposedly boards a spectral barge and, accompanied by phantom oarsmen, re-enacts her final journey by river to imprisonment in the gloomy Tower of London. Were this true, she would have left Lambeth Palace via the water gate that existed at that time, which was located in the undercroft.

Unfortunately, these tales are undermined by history. Anne did not face trial at Lambeth Palace and neither did she depart from here for the Tower of London.

In fact, Anne Boleyn was taken to the Tower from Greenwich Palace (in south-east London) on 2 May 1536, and she remained confined there until her execution only a few weeks later. Her trial, led by her uncle – Thomas Howard, Duke of Norfolk – was held inside the Tower on 15 May 1536, her brother standing trial there that same day. Both were found guilty and sentenced to death.

The basis of the Lambeth legends probably lies in the separate church court that was held at Lambeth Palace on

Morton's Tower, the Tudor gatehouse used as the main entrance into Lambeth Palace, dates back to the end of the fifteenth century.

Lambeth Palace, viewed from across the Thames.

17 May. (This was the same day on which Anne was taken to a window that looked across the Tower of London's moat and was forced to watch as her brother was beheaded on Tower Hill.) The church court at Lambeth was presided over by Archbishop Cranmer and it was this court that annulled Anne's marriage to the king, on the grounds either of Anne's earlier betrothal to the son of the Earl of Northumberland, or of the king's earlier relationship with Anne's sister, Mary. Anne herself was not present at the Lambeth Court, and news of the verdict had to be brought to her at the Tower that evening.

(I am indebted to Elizabeth Norton, author of *Anne Boleyn: In Her Own Words & the Words of Those Who Knew Her*, for the above information establishing the timeline of Anne's final days.)

Anne Boleyn was beheaded on Tower Green, within the precincts of the Tower of London, on 19 May 1536. She met her end not by the usual axe but by the sword, wielded by an executioner brought in from Calais especially for the task. (Unsurprisingly, there are many

stories of her ghost appearing in the Tower of London, and I describe these in another book: *Haunted London*.)

Anne's tale has a curious postscript. In a biography of the queen titled *Anne Boleyn*, Marie Louise Bruce writes that the Scottish reformer Alexander Aless had been staying in London on 19 May 1536, and afterwards claimed that, not having left his house, he was unaware that the queen was to be executed. Early in the morning of 19 May he awoke in terror, having seen the queen's severed head in a dream. Later that day he crossed the river to Lambeth Palace, where he met Cranmer walking in the gardens. Aless told the archbishop about his terrible vision. The archbishop listened in wonder before asking, 'Do you not know what is to happen today?' Aless replied that he did not. 'She who has been the queen of England upon earth will today become a queen in heaven,' proclaimed the archbishop. So saying, he began to weep.

More strange tales come from that part of Lambeth Palace which has become known as Lollards Tower.

The Lollards were followers of a fourteenth-century Oxford theologian named John Wycliffe, whose radical views on religion led to his being charged with heresy by the Roman Catholic Church. During the sixteenth century, Lollards were imprisoned in a small room under the roof of this tower.

'Neither Protestants nor Catholics,' wrote Thomas Pennant in *Some Account of London*, 'should omit visiting this tower, the cruel prison of the unhappy followers of Wickliffe [*sic*]. The vast staples and rings, to which they were chained before they were brought to the stake, ought to make Protestants bless the hour which freed them from so bloody a period.'

Several of these iron rings remain attached to the prison's wood-lined walls, and graffiti carved into the wood by the room's miserable occupants can also still be seen. It has been said that the misery felt by the confined Lollards lingers there too, as if the room somehow absorbed and retains the pain of their suffering.

The prison is at the top of Lollards Tower, and is reached by a narrow staircase where a supernatural presence has supposedly been felt from time to time, an invisible force that prevents people and animals from passing.

There is also said to be a door in Lambeth Palace that occasionally and for no apparent reason refuses to open. This mysterious door has been credited with saving a man's life. The story is set during a Second World War air raid, when a man on fire-watching duty climbed down a ladder from the roof. Intending to make his way to the duty-room, he tried to open the door but it refused to move, leaving him trapped for around an hour. While he was there a bomb exploded, utterly destroying the duty-room. Had the door allowed him through, the blast would certainly have killed him. (This would presumably have happened on 10 May 1941, the date on which an incendiary bomb scored a direct hit on Lambeth Palace, and much of Lollards Tower and the chapel were gutted by fire.)

In April 2008, Andrew Nunn, premises and administration secretary to the Archbishop of Canterbury, told me he had been unaware of any stories about ghosts at Lambeth Palace. He offered a down-to-earth suggestion for the story of the door, explaining that there are gaps under the modern concrete roof that, although intended for ventilation,

'Lollards Tower' in Lambeth Palace.

also let in damp. 'If any door refuses to open,' he stated, 'this will undoubtedly be the cause.'

Lambeth Palace was, in his opinion, a far less atmospheric and spooky place than the ghostly legends attached to it might suggest.

The Tomb of the Tradescants

Another Lambeth legend has it that if you dance twelve times around a certain tomb as Big Ben is striking midnight, a ghost will appear.

The tomb in question is that of the renowned Tradescant family. As well as being gardeners to royalty, John Tradescant the Elder (1570-1638) and his son, John Tradescant the Younger

(1608-1662) imported exotic plants, travelled widely, and amassed a fantastic collection of 'curiosities'. Initially focused on botanical specimens, this collection widened in scope to include all manner of interesting objects, such as animal specimens, sea shells, the 'hand of a mermaid', a small piece of wood from the True Cross of Christ, and numerous artefacts from strange cultures in distant lands. The collection inspired so much interest that it eventually opened as a museum, available to anyone who could pay the entry fee of 6d, and their house in South Lambeth came to be known as 'Tradescant's Ark'.

Right: The Garden Museum in Lambeth Palace Road.

Below: The Palace of Westminster, viewed from close to the Garden Museum. According to the legend, a ghost appears if you dance around the tomb as Big Ben chimes midnight.

The Tradescant tomb, in what used to be the churchyard of St Mary's church.

The Tradescant tomb stands in what was once the graveyard of St Mary's church. St Mary's was deconsecrated in 1972 after serving more than 900 years as the parish church of Lambeth. Afterwards the old building became increasingly derelict and it would almost certainly have been demolished eventually had it not been for the Tradescant Trust.

Formed in 1977, the Trust took over the lease, intending to create the world's first museum of garden history. The enormous task of restoring what was little more than a ruin was largely achieved thanks to voluntary contributions and today the Garden Museum in Lambeth Palace Road (close to the palace itself) is well worth a visit.

Philip Norman, volunteer curatorial assistant at the museum, has been involved with the museum for around thirty years and I am deeply grateful to him for the following details, which he passed on to me in 2008. Philip first heard of the legend attached to the Tradescant tomb during the early 1980s from an elderly man whose age Philip estimated as around ninety:

> He said when he was a small boy (so in around 1900) it was always a dare to dance around the tomb at midnight to the chimes of Big Ben to make the ghost appear, but he was too scared to do so.
>
> About fifteen years ago (in around 1993), a chap (about thirty-odd) said he did just that with his friends when he was a teenager, but as they were on their eleventh circuit, one of them let out a yelp and they scuttled off over the railings at great speed.

Memorial located opposite Tradescant Road in South Lambeth, SW8. Sculpted by Hilary Cartmel and unveiled in 1988, the plaque states that it is: 'To commemorate the Tradescant family. Plant collectors and gardeners to Charles I whose house and gardens were near this site in the seventeenth century.'

Then about three years ago (in around 2005) I heard a young boy at the garden gate shouting to his friend 'that's the grave with the ghost'.

So there is at least a 100 year tradition of the story.

Philip drew attention to a seeming inconsistency in this legend, in that it features Big Ben (the name of the bell rather than the tower, as many people mistakenly believe), which did not arrive until the mid-nineteenth century (whereas the Tradescant tomb was built long before that, in the 1660s). However, he went on to explain that the present elaborately carved tomb is not in fact the original – it too dates back to the mid-nineteenth century:

> The tomb was completely rebuilt in 1853 to the original design (now in the Pepys Library, Cambridge) that includes Hydras, a skull, crocodiles and decayed buildings.
>
> It is claimed to be the earliest representation of the Day of Judgement sculpted for a churchyard, so this may have added a twist to the tale.

Mercy Weller's Ghost

A short distance from what used to be St Mary's church (see 'The Tomb of the Tradescants'), at No. 220 Lambeth Road, stands what was once St Mary's Infant School. Built in 1880, this listed Victorian building is supposedly haunted by the ghost of its first headmistress: Mercy Weller.

Mercy shared her home at the school with her sister, Caroline Baskerville, and her sister's family. On 16 December 1887,

aged just thirty-nine, she died. She is said to have passed away in her rooms in the upstairs part of the building. After her death, the Church Commissioners refused to let Caroline take over as headmistress, and removed her (and her family) from their home.

In 1993, the old school was purchased by the Museum of Garden History (now the Garden Museum), which renamed the building 'The Ark' in honour of the Tradescant family's home. The museum used 'The Ark' for educational events, plant fairs, and to help house their library and archive.

Once again, I am indebted to Philip Norman for the following details. Although he has never encountered this ghost himself, he has collected a number of word-of-mouth accounts over the years:

> The cleaning lady we temporarily inherited with [the building] (it was a youth club) told many tales of the greyish female apparition that appeared. Her co-worker approached her one morning to ask why she'd come in through the front door (to the former headmistress's house) and [passed] the kitchen door without speaking to her – had she done something to upset her? But the cleaner responded that it certainly wasn't her. When they investigated, [they found] no one else in the building. This happened several times over the years. The figure often went outside through what was a bricked-up door.
>
> They had an electrician come to do repairs and he froze by the kitchen door saying something felt wrong, and he would not go into the house-part of the school due to a presence – so another electrician had to be called.

Above: *What was once St Mary's Infant School is supposedly haunted by the ghost of its first headmistress: Mercy Weller.*

Right: *The Victorian building's original name can be seen in this stone.*

Our first caretaker of The Ark (quite unaware of these tales), a large ex-Army chap, told me he always got funny feelings that someone was watching him – but when he turned around, no one was there. I said that was Mercy and she comes down the stairs and out through the wall, to which he replied: 'She doesn't use the stairs. I feel a chill go right down my spine when I'm sitting in my office' (in the former drawing room – bedrooms are above).

We held a botanical art class in one of the classrooms and Mercy joined in, peering over the shoulder of a student, which upset her. She hastily asked the tutor: 'Did you see her, did you see her?' Fortunately the tutor had (so she didn't feel completely mad), but none of the others in the class noticed anything.

In 2005 the museum sold the building to Fairley House School – a specialist day school for children with specific learning difficulties such as dyslexia and dyspraxia – and it became the school's Junior Department. In April 2008 Ann Osborn, head of the Junior Department, confirmed to me that she knew of the stories, but said that she had not personally encountered Mercy's presence.

The Predatory Lift of Lincoln House

At just about noon on Tuesday, 17 February 1981, two lift engineers arrived at Lincoln House, at No. 75 Westminster Bridge Road in Lambeth. Such engineers were painfully familiar with the building, having been called out to this address on numerous prior occasions, and once more they set about their all-too routine task of getting the lift machinery working again. At around 12.45 p.m., a second pair of engineers arrived. They had come to rescue the first pair, who had themselves become trapped in the notorious Lincoln House lift.

It took half an hour of hard work but eventually the trapped men were freed, the lift was working again, and all four engineers beat a hasty retreat. By 2 p.m. the Lincoln House lift had broken down again.

Lionel Beer remembers that lift only too well. He is well-used to strange stories, being one of the founding members of BUFORA (the British UFO Research Organisation) and the founder of TEMS (the Travel and Earth Mysteries Society), but during the early 1980s Lionel was working as a manager for the Central Office of Information (COI), the UK government's marketing and communications agency.

Lionel spent much of his time working in the COI's offices in Lincoln House. There he became familiar with both the capricious nature of that lift and the general feeling among his colleagues that sometimes the lift seemed almost to be alive.

He recalls the rumours – spoken not entirely in jest – that the lift's peculiar and possibly even malevolent behaviour might somehow be connected with the site's previous history. The following excerpt (reproduced with Lionel's kind permission) comes from an article he wrote for the COI's in-house magazine, *COIGN*, in 1981:

> Seriously though, folks, this has been going on for a long time, and not even the influence of two successive Directors has been able to produce lasting improvement. The amazing permutation of faults suggests that the lift has a mind of its own. While engineers have been heard to mutter darkly about bodging and fused relays, some would say that it should never have been built over a churchyard.

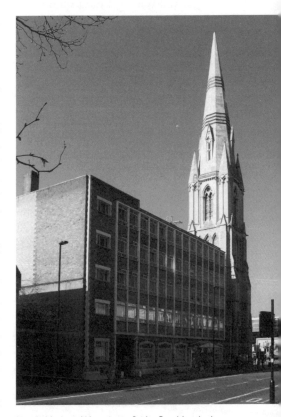

Lincoln House in Westminster Bridge Road, Lambeth.

The original Christ Church memorial stone, first laid on 26 June 1873, was salvaged after the destruction of the Second World War and can now be found at the base of the Lincoln Memorial Tower.

Lincoln House stands at the corner of Westminster Bridge Road and Kennington Road, just over the road from Lambeth North Underground station. It was built on the site of Christ Church, which was founded in the 1870s and was itself built on the site of an eighteenth-century orphanage for females. That orphanage closed at around the same time that the lease of Surrey Chapel (an independent Methodist and Congregational chapel in nearby Blackfriars Road) was due to expire. The trustees of Surrey Chapel took over the orphanage site and built a complex of buildings here that included school rooms and lecture halls, as well as the new chapel.

Also included in the plans for the site was a permanent international memorial to American President Abraham Lincoln. Funds for this memorial had been raised in America by the chapel's pastor, the Revd Dr Christopher Newman Hall, who had been an enthusiastic supporter of Lincoln's policies (in particular the abolition of slavery), and in 1874 the American ambassador laid the foundation stone for the Lincoln Memorial Tower. The tower finally opened on 4 July 1876, the centenary

of American independence. Its link to America was clearly visible in the red and white patterning of the stones in its spire: an architectural nod to the 'Stars and Stripes'.

Although the Lincoln Memorial Tower survived Hitler's bombing of London during the Second World War, the rest of the Christ Church complex was destroyed. During the 1950s and '60s the damaged site was redeveloped, following which the dramatic, Gothic-revival architecture of the tower was left standing – somewhat incongruously – besides a large, modernist office building. Despite its functional exterior, the office building incorporated a new chapel – a combined Congregational and Baptist chapel known as 'Christ Church and Upton Chapel'. This had been built to replace both Christ Church and a Baptist church called Upton Hall, which had

The tower's connection with the USA is visible in the red and white patterning of the stones in its spire – an architectural version of the 'Stars and Stripes' of the American flag.

stood on Lambeth Road and had also been destroyed during the war.

In more recent years, the site's identity has continued to evolve. In June 2003, Christ Church and Upton Chapel entered a partnership with the Oasis Trust, creating a united church called 'Church.co.uk, Waterloo'. (According to the latter's website, the Oasis Trust aims 'to provide and support education, housing, health care and employment across the world, as well as support and leadership to local churches.') In 2011, the church became 'Oasis Church, Waterloo'.

Returning to the story of the Lincoln House lift, and to the persecuted employees working in that unusual dual-purpose modernist office block on the site of the destroyed Christ Church, the following excerpt is taken from the same article as before:

Christ Church and Upton Chapel, somewhat incongruously incorporated into the modernist office building.

> ... let the official statistics speak for themselves. [The] records show that between 15 October 1980 and 14 January 1981, the lift engineers were called to remedy faults on nineteen occasions. On five of these occasions, people were actually trapped in the lift as a result of a fault. A further breakdown occurred on 29 January when two people were trapped adjacent to the fifth floor. A visitor to Lincoln House was trapped on the third floor on 11 March and so it went on until the Spring Bank Holiday weekend, when some major repairs were carried out. Subsequently, stoppages have been fewer.

Breakdowns were not the only problem. What Lionel Beer called this 'devilish piece of machinery' also had an unsettling habit of ignoring the instructions it was given, choosing instead to transport its helpless occupants all the way down to the basement. Lionel remembers that there was a lingering 'bad feeling' down there, as close to the original church ground as it was possible to get. In 2009 he told me about one particular occasion on which he himself was carried unwillingly to the basement. As far as he can remember, this probably happened during 1981.

'I still recall wondering if my number was up when the lift took me to the basement of Lincoln House, and would not release me,' he said.

His worry stemmed not so much from the alarming prospect of being trapped in that lift for the rest of the night, as from the fact that the cleaners had evidently spilled some chemicals in or near the lift shortly beforehand. The spill had caused fumes to build in the confined space, fumes that now grew thicker and more choking the longer Lionel remained trapped in his metal cell. Very quickly, it became difficult to breathe.

41

The Necropolis Railway's London terminus was originally located at York Street. This is now Leake Street, where the graffiti-decorated walls of the 'Banksy Tunnel' run below the tracks and platforms of Waterloo station.

Frantically, he pressed the button to summon help. It took around half an hour for him to be rescued, but fortunately he was eventually freed, feeling 'groggy' from the fumes but otherwise unharmed.

Was there ever really a connection between the lift's mutinous behaviour and the fact that Lincoln House had been built on holy ground, or were such rumours simply the result of failing machinery mixed with idle office gossip and a smattering of interesting local history? No one will ever know for certain now.

One day the lift's unlucky prey consisted of a group of visiting VIPs. Although these highly important personages were eventually freed from the lift's clutches, the embarrassing fallout from this incident probably helped speed along the overdue decision to give the entire system a proper overhaul.

And that was that. In mid-1981 the lift was at long last condemned, the decision

to pay for a brand-new system was given an official rubber stamp, and the unsettlingly self-minded lift of Lincoln House was deprived of any further victims.

The Lingering Shadow of Waterloo's Necropolis Railway

The question of what to do with the dead plagued London during the first half of the nineteenth century. Between 1801 and 1851 the metropolitan population more than doubled, rising from around 1 million to over 2.25 million, and as the number of living rapidly increased so did the number of the dying. London no longer had space to accommodate all the burials it needed.

The results were horrific. What had been intended as final resting places were desecrated and reused; bones from previous inhabitants were taken away to be crushed and used as fertiliser; poor families used the wood from unearthed coffins for fuel; and the sale of second-hand 'coffin furniture' provided a grim source of income for those hard-hearted – or desperate – enough not to respect the sanctity of burial. And then there were the health problems caused by all the decaying remains polluting London's water supplies. Something had to be done.

One proposed solution to this macabre congestion was to build a vast new cemetery, one large enough to accommodate all of London's burials for the foreseeable future. To allow room for London's continuing expansion, it was decided to locate this new 'Necropolis' at Brookwood, near Woking in Surrey – approximately 23 miles south-west of the city. Travel to and from this remote cemetery was to exploit the recently developed technology of railway transport, using special funeral trains to carry coffins and mourners via a dedicated station near Waterloo.

The plan went ahead and Brookwood Cemetery was consecrated on 7 November 1854, with the first funeral trains beginning to run the following week. For most of the route the trains steamed their way along existing tracks belonging to the London and South Western Railway (LSWR).

Originally, the London terminus for the Necropolis train service was located at York Street (now Leake Street) in Lambeth. By the end of the nineteenth century, however, the LSWR wanted to improve and enlarge its own facilities at Waterloo, and to do so would involve demolition of the York Street station. After much discussion, an agreement was reached between the LSWR and the London Necropolis Co., and a new London terminus for the funeral train service was built in Westminster Bridge Road. This opened to the public in 1902.

The Westminster Bridge Road station operated until the Second World War when, during an air raid on the night of 16-17 April 1941, it was badly damaged by bombing. Although the platforms, First Class waiting rooms and office building survived, most of the station was destroyed. It was officially declared closed a few weeks later.

After the war, the London Necropolis Co. lacked the will to rebuild the station and reinstate the funeral train service. Despite its sombre trappings,

This used to be the Westminster Bridge Road entrance to the Necropolis Railway.

Photographed in 2012, these iron columns beside Newnham Terrace once supported the Necropolis platforms and tracks.

In January 2007, a short report was submitted to the 'Paranormal Database' website. The gentleman who sent it in explained that one particular part of the railway training school, known as 'A Block', had consisted of a long corridor with classrooms arranged along either side. 'During the evenings or at weekends,' he claimed, 'when the buildings were quiet, classroom and other doors could be heard slamming – to the extent that some staff refused to work alone in the building.' He gave the date for these happenings as '1990 onwards'.

The 'Paranormal Database' owner, Darren Mann, kindly tried to get in touch with this gentleman in 2011 to obtain further information on my behalf, but his contact details proved to be out of date. However, in January 2012 users of the 'RailUK Forums' internet discussion site helpfully confirmed to me that the story of a haunting at the training school was indeed circulating during the 1990s, although details remain hazy.

One correspondent recalled that the site had already been in a fairly run-down state while he was there during the

the company had always been intended as a commercial venture and it had hoped to gain a monopoly of London's burial industry; ultimately, however, it had failed to do so. Even taking into account the compensation it would receive from the War Damage Commission, the cost of repairing the Westminster Bridge Road facilities and replacing the damaged or destroyed railway stock was deemed too high, and in September 1945 the directors concluded that 'past experience and present changed conditions made the running of the private train obsolete.' In December 1946 it was agreed that ownership of the railway portions of the site (the platforms, waiting rooms, and the caretaker's flat) would return to what was now the Southern Railway (SR), while everything else was to be sold or let by the London Necropolis Co.

By the 1960s the old Necropolis platforms had become home to a railway training school housed within various prefabricated buildings. At least some of the staff, and some of those undergoing their training here, knew of the site's unusual and rather morbid history, and so it is perhaps unsurprising that rumours emerged that there was something eerie about this school.

In 2010 the abandoned railway training school became home to artists' studios. (Photograph courtesy of Make Space Studios, Newnham Terrace, London, SE1 7DR: www.makespacestudios.com)

late 1970s/early '80s, although he could not remember having heard of this ghost story during his time there.

Another, who had often attended training courses and meetings there during the early 1990s, did remember hearing that the school was supposed to be haunted. Although he had never experienced anything himself, or met anyone who had, he said that he could 'imagine the place being a little spooky on a dark evening if you were on your own!'

A third correspondent (who had worked there as a contractor to Railtrack in the late 1990s) stated that most of the offices had become empty by 1999, although the school was still being used for training. 'I was never there at night time,' he said, 'as even during the daytime it was quiet!'

Although the obvious inspiration for rumours of a haunting here is the site's past history as the Necropolis station, another possibility was suggested to me by John Clarke, an expert on the railway's history and the author of *The Brookwood Necropolis Railway*. (This excellent book is highly recommended to readers who would like to find out more about the fascinating history of the Necropolis railway.)

Clarke (no relation to the present author!) told me that on the night of 14 March 1929, a twenty-two-year-old police constable named David Ford was searching for a burglar when he (Ford) fell through a plate-glass canopy over the station's Third Class platform. PC Ford died at the scene. Those inclined to paranormal explanations might speculate that the reported sound of slamming doors was a ghostly echo of PC Ford opening and shutting doors during his search on that fateful night.

By the early years of the twenty-first century the school had fallen into disuse but in January 2010, after lying empty for at least three years, the old grey buildings were given a colourful makeover and brought back to life by 'Make Space Studios'. As at the beginning of 2012, the site is a vibrant home to more than seventy artists' studios, and the rumours of a ghost have been left to the past.

Ghosts at The Old Vic

A short walk east of Waterloo station stands one of England's oldest surviving theatre buildings: The Old Vic. First opened in May 1818 as the Royal Coburg Theatre, it was renamed the Royal Victoria Theatre in 1833, in honour of Princess (and later Queen) Victoria. For a time its fortunes fluctuated, and by 1880 it had become the Royal Victoria Coffee and Music Hall, 'a cheap and decent place of amusement' run on 'strict temperance lines' by the social reformer Emma Cons. When Emma died in 1912, the management was taken over by her niece, Lilian Baylis, and under her leadership The Old Vic became one of the country's

The foundation stone in the Webber Street wall of the theatre: 'This first stone of the Royal Coburg Theatre was laid on the 14th day of September in the year 1816 by His Serene Highness the Prince of Saxe-Coburg and Her Royal Highness Princess Charlotte of Wales by Their Serene and Royal Highnesss [sic] proxy Alderman Goodbehere.'

Left: *Baylis Road, opposite The Old Vic, named in honour of Lilian Baylis.*

Below: *The Old Vic is one of England's oldest surviving theatre buildings.*

leading theatres, widely renowned for its Shakespearean productions.

When Lilian Baylis died in 1937, the play *Macbeth* was about to open at the theatre. It is with that supposedly cursed play that the building's best-known ghost story is associated. The Old Vic is reputedly haunted (or at least, is reputed to have been haunted during its early years) by the apparition of a distressed woman, wringing together her blood-stained hands. The woman's identity is unknown but it is usually claimed that the spectacle is of an actress playing the part of Lady Macbeth and that the blood is therefore stage blood. Traditionally, the apparition is said to be the actress' restless spirit, compelled for some reason

to replay her role over and over again, although another suggestion has been that the sight represents some sort of paranormal recording of a long-ago performance of 'the Scottish play'.

In 2008 stage-door manager Ned Seago confirmed to me that he had heard this story, although he did not know anyone who had personally witnessed the apparition. He did, however, tell me of his own eerie experience in the theatre one night, and I am grateful to him for allowing his account to be included here:

I wish I could say it begins with, 'It was a dark and stormy night,' but alas, it was a pacific, late evening in August 1989.

As one of the stage-door keepers I lock the door at the end of the evening before leaving the reception area to lock up the interior of the building: dressing room, offices, etc. from the third floor, clockwise, downward. On this particular evening I had secured the top floor and encountered nobody. I was at the far end of the second-floor corridor when I saw, through the small window in the door at my end of the corridor, someone through the window of the far door. There are staircases at either side of the building and it is therefore possible for two people to wander around without meeting each other at all, and I supposed that the person I had just seen was one of the Hungarian Company that The Old Vic was hosting as part of the LIFT (London International Festival of Theatre) celebrations. Naturally, as the stage door was locked, I had to descend to let the person (I had the impression that it was female) out of the building. I came back across the corridor and down the stairs, and just as I came through the door at stage level, above ground level, that person disappeared through the bricked-up doorway just inside the stage door. Clearly she was not a Hungarian actress! If anyone, I'd like to think it was Lilian Baylis.

Perhaps it really was the ghost of Lilian Baylis. According to The Old Vic website, during the final performance there by the National Theatre Company in 1976, before they moved to their new home on the South Bank, Peggy Ashcroft played the role of Lilian Baylis in Tribute to the Lady, and in her curtain speech she quoted Baylis' 'threat to come back and haunt The Old Vic should her

and her aunt Emma Cons' work ever be put at risk.' Perhaps Lilian did indeed return to watch over her beloved theatre.

In his 1988 book Theatre Ghosts, Roy Harley Lewis records another story of someone returning to The Old Vic after death. Shortly after the First World War, a promising young actor named Eric Ross was due to play the part of Brutus in a production of Julius Caesar. Before the play opened, however, four cast members were struck down with Spanish Flu and three of them, including Eric, died. Finding actors to replace them was difficult – many actors had been killed in the war, and many others remained in service – but replacements were eventually found and the play was able to go ahead.

On its opening night, however, several members of the audience were reportedly puzzled by the presence on stage of one particular figure, a man who, during the orchard scene, seemed to stand apart from the conspirators, as if he did not really belong to that group. Those audience members who noticed the figure were willing to make allowances for a late replacement: perhaps the man hadn't had time to learn the staging. However, when the play's director, George R. Foss, heard these comments he was confused: he hadn't noticed anyone standing apart from the main group. Foss grew even more confused when he questioned further people – it became clear that only some had seen this extra actor. At least one member of the audience felt that the extra actor, visible to only some of the gathered crowd, had been none other than Eric Ross returning to the stage, in spirit form, to ensure the opening night's performance went well.

4

AROUND NORWOOD

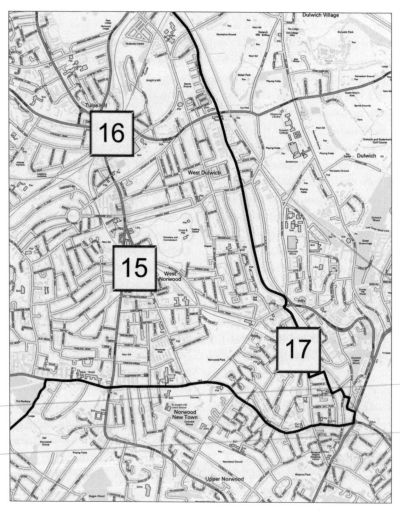

AROUND NORWOOD. *Key: (15) The Ghost of Norwood; (16) Tulse Hill Station and the Phantom Footsteps of Platform One; (17) Gipsy Hill: Fortune Tellers and a Headless Phantom. (Contains Ordnance Survey data © Crown copyright and database right 2012.)*

The Ghost of Norwood

In July 1951, local newspapers started to report unusual events at No. 5 Langmead Street, a small council house in a tiny road tucked away to the south of West Norwood train station. The houses here have since been demolished and, as of 2012, commercial premises occupy the road.

Since 1947, the house had been home to the Greenfield family: Augustus Greenfield, a sixty-nine-year-old employee of Lambeth Council; Mrs Greenfield, his sixty-year-old wife; and their sons Cecil, twenty-six, and Dennis, twenty-two, and a fourteen-year-old daughter, Pat. Also living in the house in 1951 were Dennis's twenty-year-old wife, Gladys; Gladys's mother; and an eight-year-old boy named Gordon (it is not completely clear in the reports whether he was brother to Cecil, Dennis and Pat). All in all, this meant that a grand total of eight occupants squeezed into the house's six small rooms.

The Greenfields had been experiencing unusual incidents on and off for at least a few months leading up to that July. The first signs of anything odd had been sounds of soft tapping coming from the false ceiling above the top floor. Initially they assumed that birds or rodents were responsible, yet inspection of the empty loft area revealed no evidence of animals.

To begin with, the tapping – although it must have been irritating – was not very loud and could only be heard by someone on the floor immediately below the loft. Over time, however, the noises grew louder, until eventually they could be clearly heard from anywhere in the house. Too loud now to be blamed on small animals, the noises sounded as if someone were walking around in – or dragging furniture across – the loft.

The only way to get to the loft was by a ladder on the floor below. This made the loft inaccessible to anyone who did not live in the house – yet despite this, Dennis and Gladys discovered mysterious marks up there one night. Dennis later described this incident to the *Norwood News*, and he was quoted in the 20 July edition as saying:

> I was in my room with my wife when we heard footsteps overhead in the attic. We went up, but found nobody. Yet the dust had been disturbed, and there were initials, 'A.T.', and two circles, as though written by a finger. We went down and stayed in our parents' room until 5 a.m., but back in our room we discovered beds neatly made which had been untidy when we left them.

At other times the Greenfields heard sounds of footsteps on the stairs.

Langmead Street in 2012. In the mid-twentieth century, one of the small council houses that used to stand here was home to the 'Ghost of Norwood'.

There were also reports of strange lights being seen: Mrs Nellie Green, a neighbour who lived opposite the house, said that she had seen a light moving slowly up and down at one of the Greenfields' top-floor windows during the night of Wednesday 11 July.

At first the disturbances took place only at night, but after a while things began to happen during daylight hours as well. One day, two wooden boxes that had been left unattended in a corner of the sitting room were found on a chair. Inconsequential as such incidents might appear in isolation, their inexplicability gnawed away at the family's nerves. By the middle of July the family was so worried that Cecil Greenfield contacted the police.

'I was sceptical when I received a report of the matter,' Inspector Sidney Candler later told the *Norwood News*, 'but after interviewing the Greenfields I am convinced something strange has happened at the house, something which calls for police investigation.'

Candler arranged for some of his colleagues to stay with the family for a while. On the night of Friday 13 July, two CID men and a neighbour, seventeen-year-old Robert Green, stayed up with members of the Greenfield family to try to discover what was going on. Despite the ominous date, the night began quietly. When nothing had happened by 3 a.m., the detectives left. Just a quarter of an hour after their departure a policeman in a patrol car outside heard moaning and went to investigate. He found Cecil, Dennis, Gladys and Robert Green on the top floor, pale with fright. 'It was horrible,' recalled Green afterwards. 'We heard moans and a scratching noise. Then, near the skirting board, we saw what

looked like an electric bulb glowing.' The glowing light was apparently similar to that seen two nights earlier by Nellie Green.

That Saturday the Greenfields went out in the afternoon, locking the front door behind them. When they returned home later they discovered that the hallway mirror had been turned to face the wall.

At about 1 a.m. on Sunday 15 July, as one police officer stood watch on the street outside, guarding the bolted front door, a second police officer, who was keeping vigil with the family inside the house, heard bumping and tapping noises coming from the loft. He climbed up to investigate but found nothing there.

A few minutes later, in one of the bedrooms, an eiderdown that Gladys was certain had been left at the foot of the bed was found at the head of the bed. Keeping a clear head, the police officer instructed everyone to gather in the sitting room and remain there while he sat on the bed. Then they all waited to see if anything further would occur. Approximately twenty minutes later there was a loud crash from the sitting room. A picture that had been hanging by a strong cord from a nail had fallen to the floor. The nail was still firmly in place in the wall, and the cord had not broken.

On Monday morning (16 July) an apparition was seen. Cecil awoke during the early hours, thinking he had heard someone moving around outside his bedroom on the first floor. He got up and opened the bedroom door. The landing was empty. Wondering if someone was feeling ill and had gone downstairs to the kitchen, he decided to take a look – but as he did so he saw something coming up the stairs towards him. It was a greyish-white, human-shaped figure, approximately 6ft tall. He did not notice any facial details.

It drew closer, and as it approached Cecil felt increasingly cold (possibly due to his mounting terror). There was a creak as the figure passed over a loose floorboard on the stairs, as if the apparition had physically stepped there. Still it approached, drawing nearer and nearer, and now it was practically upon him. Cecil screamed – and the moment he did so the figure vanished.

Recalling this incident a short time later, Dennis was quoted in the *Norwood News* (Friday 20 July) as saying: 'He [Cecil] yelled, and when I rushed upstairs I found him sitting on his bed as white as a sheet and trembling. He is so terrified that he will not go upstairs alone – and he is twenty-six years old.'

For sixty-year-old Mrs Greenfield the weekend was all too much. Her husband had already approached Lambeth Council to ask for the family to be re-housed, but she could bear the situation no longer and went to stay with relatives.

At around midday on Monday, according to the *South London Press* of 17 July: 'while the family were cooking their dinner and the house swarmed with reporters, photographers and investigators, a tea caddy fell off the table. No one was near it. A picture also moved.' With admirable understatement, an exasperated Augustus Greenfield was quoted as saying: 'This is getting on our nerves.'

The same day, the cryptic message 'M P S 238' (or possibly 'M P S Z38') was found scratched on the wall of an upstairs room.

That afternoon Mrs Hilda Bussley, a daughter of Mr and Mrs Greenfield

On the morning of Monday, 16 July 1951 Cecil Greenfield encountered a greyish-white apparition coming up the stairs towards him. (© Anthony Wallis: www.ant-wallis-illustration.blogspot.co.uk.)

who no longer lived at home, visited the house. She claimed that when she walked into her mother's bedroom she heard 'heavy breathing coming from the vacant bed'.

By now, news of the disturbances was exciting considerable interest in the neighbourhood. The day before, local children at the Sunday School had been interested only in garnering their teacher's opinions on the 'ghost' in Langmead Street. As Monday went on, matters began to get out of hand. That afternoon (or early that evening) groups of children gathered outside the house; there were boos and catcalls, and stones were thrown at the Greenfields' door and windows. In the evening, a larger and older crowd gathered to gawp at the house in the hope of seeing something exciting. The crowd grew so oppressive that Augustus was forced to call the police again for help and squad cars were sent to move the onlookers away.

Inside, the strange activity continued. During the night of Tuesday 17 July two 'kiss marks' were found on the glass of a wardrobe, and a crucifix on a dressing table was turned upside down. At around midnight, the Greenfields decided to abandon their home temporarily, choosing to spend the rest of that night with friends.

Other phenomena that had also been reported by now include the following: radios would switch on by themselves; books were found torn and scattered around; vegetables and assorted kitchen items moved independently to a bedroom; a shopping basket in an empty room moved to the opposite side of the room; a photograph fell out of its frame, even though the glass front and the backing remained undisturbed; and there were flashes of bright light in a downstairs room. Once, Dennis claimed that he saw a bottle of milk moving upstairs by itself, one step at a time!

Some of the reports sound quite alarming. Young Gordon was seemingly thrown down the stairs by some mysterious force, although he was unharmed by the incident. On another occasion, Dennis walked into his sister Pat's bedroom to see her mattress 'lifting and curling up' as if an invisible being were holding it. As the mattress hung in the air, Dennis grabbed and tugged at it but found that he could not move it – and then he felt as if something briefly grabbed him from behind.

A few days after its first appearance, the apparition was seen again. Dennis and Gladys returned home in the early hours of the morning, having been to a party, and as they opened the front door and walked into the hallway they saw a greyish-white figure standing there, motionless. It seemed to be the same figure as that described by Cecil earlier; as before, no facial details could be made out. Terrified, the couple ran to a neighbour's house. When they returned, a short while later, the figure had gone.

Pat also saw the apparition one afternoon as she made her way down the stairs. 'She was coming down with my mother-in-law,' said Dennis, 'when she stopped and started screaming. Yet my mother-in-law did not see a thing.'

Various people attempted to deal with what became known as the 'Ghost of Norwood'.

Throughout the week beginning Monday 16 July, a Mission Band held services in Langmead Street, close to the house, and a number of spiritualists and religious leaders came forward to offer their assistance in 'laying the ghost'.

The Revd John Crouch, minister of the Church of the Nazarene in nearby Auckland Hill, visited Langmead Street with members of his congregation and held a service outside the Greenfields' home. 'It was just before 10 p.m., when one of the young Greenfields came out and invited us into their home to pray,' Crouch told the Norwood News afterwards. 'Seven of our party went in, and in the front room we knelt with the assembled family and there prayed, finally commanding the Thing to "leave this house in the name of the Lord Jesus Christ".' Crouch was satisfied that his efforts had helped to resolve the situation.

Also lending his services to the beleaguered family was Mr W.E. Brookson, a medium from Brixton, who attempted to make contact with the ghost as the Greenfields looked on. Brookson was aided by his secretary, who the *South London Press* later quoted as stating: 'It seems that the ghost is 400 years old. He buried something under the house. He has been worrying about it. Whatever it was, I believe we have succeeded in persuading him to go away.'

Despite all the efforts to get rid of it, however, the ghost remained well and truly alive in the public mind, if only as a source of amusement. On Saturday 28 July, the nearby St Matthew's church held a fête in the grounds of St Joseph's Primary School, Crown Dale, Upper Norwood. The popular actor Derek Guyler had been scheduled to open the event but, as he could not attend, Father Cole of St Matthew's announced to the crowds waiting on that hot afternoon that a last-minute replacement had been found.

'I got in touch with the Infernal Regions,' joked Father Cole, 'but was informed that he [the ghost] never made a personal appearance except at midnight. "But I want you to come along and open our fête at 3 p.m.," I said, and the ghost replied, "I'll come along and open it but the people will not see me".'

Father Cole then introduced his surprise guest, and the crowds heard a muffled voice from the speakers say: 'Here I am, hope it's a nice afternoon.' And with that, the resourceful priest declared the fête well and truly 'opened by the Norwood Ghost'!

Discounting the ghost's 'appearance' at the fête, it did seem, at first, that the attempts to exorcise it had been successful, at least according to an article in the spiritualist newspaper *The Two Worlds* on 11 August 1951. Referring to the service performed by Revd Crouch,

this article commented: 'Whether the service provided a good excuse for some practical joker to cease his pranks, or whether an evil entity was really banished by the prayers, is difficult to judge.' Crouch himself tended to believe that the disturbances had been the work of a malevolent spirit and he was convinced that his prayers had been instrumental in bringing peace to the Greenfields' home.

Unfortunately, by the time this article appeared in print it was already out of date. Other newspaper reports suggest that the ghost returned to the house in Langmead Street during the Bank Holiday Weekend of Saturday 4 August to Monday 6 August. By now, though, the battle-hardened Greenfields were less fazed by its antics. Mrs Greenfield senior was quoted in the *Norwood News* (10 August 1951) as saying: 'It came again on Tuesday (7 August) and did such silly things. Upstairs it piled the furniture on my son's bed, and then it put a broken clothes peg in a bottle and put it on the landing.' She added, with a smile: 'I can't see the sense of things like that, can you?'

Mrs Greenfield said that the family knew whenever the ghost was around because:

> ... the place goes dull and the glass in the pictures goes all misty ... and we hear noises, like someone walking overhead. Sure enough, when we got upstairs, there are the things we left, all upset and awry ... so we don't sleep upstairs any more; we just let the Thing get on with it ... and we say what we think about it out loud.

Her daughter Pat confirmed to the *Norwood News'* reporter that the family no longer spent the nights in their bedrooms, instead sitting together in one of the downstairs rooms, adding that despite the nuisance they were determinedly 'sticking it out'.

Mrs Greenfield senior commented that Pat often spoke aloud to the ghost, asking why it didn't use its powers for useful purposes, such as helping to wash the dishes! 'It does not take the hint,' she said, 'but we are not worried about it any more, it can do as it pleases.'

Despite their humour, the family did still want to be rid of their uninvited houseguest and said they were waiting for a gentleman from the 'Psychical Society' to return from his holiday. Upon his return Mrs Greenfield senior intended to ask him to arrange for 'a prominent medium to come and ask it what it wants, then, when it has got it, perhaps it will go away.'

Eventually the ghost – or whatever it was – did go away, although whether or not this was thanks to the 'prominent medium' does not seem to have been reported in the newspapers. It is quite probable that there never was any definitive resolution to the affair, and that the puzzling happenings simply tailed off gradually, fading away in the way that poltergeist cases tend to, leaving behind only a sense of bewilderment and the age-old, unanswered question: 'Well, what was all that about then?'

Two years after the affair of the 'Norwood Ghost', the house in Langmead Street became home to new occupants: Mr and Mrs Hewitt and their four young children, who lived untroubled by any apparitions, weird noises or mysteriously shifting furniture.

The haunting in Langmead Street was investigated at the time by ghost researcher Philip Paul, who initially wondered whether the Greenfields might have been claiming to have a poltergeist simply to get the council to re-house them. After interviewing them, however, Paul came to believe that they were telling the truth, although he retained doubts as to the reality of all the reported phenomena. In *The Encyclopedia of Ghosts and Spirits*, authors John and Anne Spencer note that Paul was of the opinion that some of Dennis's claims were 'probably hallucinatory after the periods of strain he had been under', although he did not believe that the claims contained any deliberate fakery.

Inspector Candler, too, came away from the case believing that something strange had been going on in that house. Years afterwards, the policeman admitted to Philip Paul that he remained baffled by the events.

Tulse Hill Station and the Phantom Footsteps of Platform One

Tulse Hill train station first opened in 1868 as part of the London, Brighton and South Coast Railway's line from London Bridge. Few of the passengers that pass through this busy station today realise it is supposedly haunted by a dead man's footsteps.

An unknown number of years ago, Porter W.J. 'Bill' Caulfield was on night duty. The last train had just pulled out of the station, and as the few passengers trudged homeward Caulfield locked the gate behind them. Then he retired to the warmth of the porters' room on number one platform, where he soon dozed off.

Before long he was awoken by the sound of heavy boots on a hard stone

Left: *Is Tulse Hill train station haunted by the sound of a dead man's footsteps?*

Below: *Platform one of Tulse Hill station.*

surface. The footsteps seemed to be coming from the steps leading to the gate outside and presumably belonged to a maintenance man arriving to carry out some work on the track. Caulfield fully expected that the man would call out for the gate to be opened – but no call came.

Instead, the footsteps continued to approach steadily, closer and closer, and now the sound changed, no longer that of boots on stone but of boots on the wooden boards of the platform, on this side of the securely locked gate.

Caulfield took his lantern from the table and walked out onto the platform to see who was there. He could still hear the deliberate tread of footsteps, walking away from him now, across the darkened platform and towards the track, yet no matter how hard he strained his eyes

he could see nobody. He quickly lit all the gas-lamps and searched every room of the station but nowhere did he find any trace of a visitor. Confused, and a little nervous, he returned to the porters' room, locked the door behind him, and stayed shut in there until morning came and his shift finished.

Back at home, Caulfield slept off the odd incident, and by the next time he was scheduled for night duty he had almost forgotten about what had happened. After locking the station for the night, he settled down for a snooze in the porters' room – but he was soon awoken once again by the sound of heavy footsteps on the station's stone steps.

As before, the footsteps seemed to pass straight through the locked gate without missing a beat. They approached, ever closer, across the platform, until at last whoever was responsible must have been standing right outside the door to the porters' room. There the footsteps paused. Inside, Caulfield listened, wondering what was about to happen. Then the footsteps resumed, moving away across the wooden platform and on, down the ramp at the platform end before crunching onto the track.

Caulfield seized his lantern and dashed outside. He made a thorough search of the platform and every one of the station buildings, and looked up and down the track for any sign of an intruder. Just as before, there was nobody to be seen.

A few weeks later, Caulfield was working an afternoon shift. He had told nobody about the mysterious footsteps in case he was laughed at, but when he took his break in the porters' room and found several members of staff and the station foreman drinking mugs of tea and swapping work-related anecdotes he decided the time had come. As casually as possible, he told his tale.

'There, what did I tell you?' said the foreman, when Caulfield finished. 'Almost word for word what happened to me!'

Apparently, Caulfield had not been the first person to hear the ghostly footsteps at Tulse Hill station. Moreover, the foreman – who had worked there a long time – was able to offer a background to the phenomenon and he told the story of a tragic accident that had occurred many years before, in the days when steam locomotives were just beginning to give way to the new electric trains.

On the night in question, a gale had been blowing when a platelayer (a worker who inspects and maintains the tracks) climbed the steps to number one platform, walked past the porters' room and stepped down onto the tracks. Aware that a steam train was expected on the down track, he took care to keep between the rails of the up track. The steam locomotive duly approached – and between its powerful roar and the violence of the rushing wind, the platelayer did not hear the sound of the relatively quiet electric train that ran into him from behind and killed him.

The story recounted above was recorded by Jack Hallam in his *Ghosts of London*, published in 1975. No dates were given for any of the events, but the line in question was electrified in 1912, which does suggest an approximate date for the accident described.

Gipsy Hill: Fortune Tellers and a Headless Phantom

The area known as Gipsy Hill in the south-eastern corner of Lambeth borough takes its name from the Norwood Gipsies who lived around here for centuries. They became especially famous during the seventeenth and eighteenth centuries, when their reputation for occult powers attracted countless visitors who wanted to know what the future held for them. Most famous of their number was Margaret Finch – 'The Queen of the Norwood Gipsies' – who, it is claimed, lived to the impressive age of 108 or 109.

In his *History and Antiquities of the Parish of Lambeth* (1827), Thomas Allen wrote of Margaret Finch:

After travelling over various parts of the kingdom during the greater part

Echoes of the past: the area's long association with the Norwood Gipsies surfaces in many local place names, as these examples show.

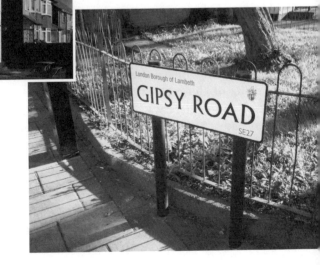

Above: A headless phantom is said to walk the darkness of the Crystal Palace Tunnel, viewed here from outside Crystal Palace train station.

Left: Gipsy Hill train station.

of a century, she settled at Norwood; whither her great age, and the fame of her fortune-telling, attracted numerous visitors. From a habit of sitting on the ground with her chin resting on her knees, the sinews at length became so contracted that she could not rise from that posture; after her death they were obliged to enclose her body in a deep square box. She was buried in Beckenham Church-yard, Oct. 24, 1740.

The area changed greatly during the latter half of the nineteenth century, as its population rapidly increased after the opening of Gipsy Hill train station in 1856. The line here was owned by the West End of London and Crystal Palace Railway, although it was operated by the London, Brighton and South Coast Railway.

Next time you find yourself standing on the platform at Gipsy Hill station, waiting for a train that will take you out of Lambeth borough and towards Crystal Palace, turn your gaze south-east along the line and think about the tunnel that lies ahead. It is said that 'many years ago' a platelayer working here was accidentally hit by a train and decapitated. (See 'Tulse Hill Station and the Phantom Footsteps of Platform One' for a similar ghost story.) His phantom – usually said to be headless – reputedly wanders through the darkness of the Crystal Palace Tunnel, the long, black tunnel you will pass through a few minutes after your train departs.

5

AROUND STOCKWELL

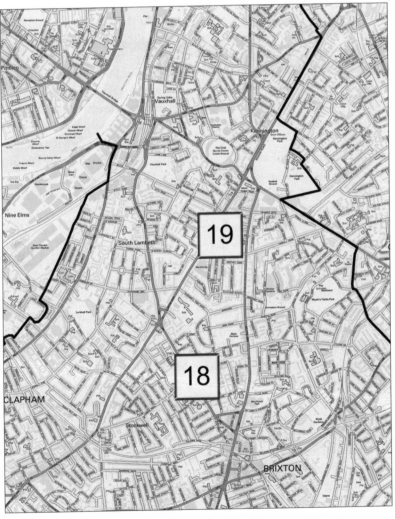

AROUND STOCKWELL. *Key: (18) The Stockwell Ghost; (19) A Ghost on the Northern Line.
(Contains Ordnance Survey data © Crown copyright and database right 2012.)*

The Stockwell Ghost

The notorious affair of the 'Stockwell Ghost' began on the morning of Monday 6 January 1772. At first it seemed to be the work of some devilish spirit.

A detailed written account of what happened was made very soon afterwards and was signed by the principal witnesses just a few days later, on 11 January. The quotations that appear below are taken from that tract, which was succinctly titled: *An authentic, candid, and circumstantial narrative of the astonishing transactions at Stockwell, in the county of Surrey, on Monday and Tuesday, the 6th and 7th days of January, 1772, containing a series of the most surprising and unaccountable events that ever happened; which continued from first to last upwards of twenty hours, and at different places.*

Based on information in a newspaper article titled 'Kennington and Stockwell in the 18th Century' and thought to date from the late nineteenth or early twentieth centuries, the house where these events occurred appears to have stood in Stockwell Road, probably more or less opposite Stockwell Green.

The house was home to Mrs Golding, 'an elderly lady of independent fortune' who lived there with her maid, Ann Robinson. Ann, who was aged about twenty, had only been with Mrs Golding for a week and three days when the disturbances began.

At about 10 a.m., Mrs Golding was in her parlour when she heard a noise from the back kitchen. The maid rushed in to say that plates were falling from the shelf and Mrs Golding went to the kitchen to find them in pieces on the floor. As she stood there a row of plates from the next shelf suddenly fell to the ground, and then 'other things in different places began to tumble about, some of them breaking, attended with violent noises all over the house; a clock tumbled down and the case broke; a lanthorn that hung on the staircase was thrown down and the glass broke to pieces; an earthen pan of salted beef broke to pieces and the beef fell about.'

Unnerved, Mrs Golding asked some neighbours to come to the house. One, a carpenter named Mr Rowlidge, opined that the 'foundation was giving way and that the house was tumbling down, occasioned by the too great weight of an additional room erected above'. It soon became apparent, however, that this was not the explanation because the commotion clearly followed Mrs Golding and her maid wherever they went and ceased as soon as they left a room.

By now thoroughly frightened, Mrs Golding hurried next door to the house of a gentleman named Mr Gresham. There she fainted. The neighbours, fearing for her health, sent for her niece (who lived in Brixton Causeway with her husband, a farmer named Mr Pain). By the time Mrs Pain arrived at Mr Gresham's house, Mrs Golding had recovered somewhat, although she was still feeling faint.

Now things started to happen in Mr Gresham's house: 'The glasses and china which stood on the side-board, began to tumble about and fall down, and broke both the glasses to pieces. Mr Saville and others being asked to drink a glass of wine or rum, both the bottles broke in pieces before they were uncorked.'

In a state of 'confused chaos', Mrs Golding could see no way out of the strange hell in which she found herself. It seemed that wherever she and

Stockwell Road in 2012, looking north from opposite Moat Place: in 1772 Mrs Golding's house would probably have stood a short distance ahead, on the right.

Stockwell Road in 2012, looking south from opposite Stockwell Lane: Mrs Golding's house would probably have stood a short distance ahead, on the left.

her maid went, these 'strange destructive circumstances' would follow them. She left Mr Gresham's home and went to the next house along. This belonged to a gentleman named Mr Mayling and Mrs Golding must have thought she had finally escaped because, while she was there, she enjoyed a brief respite from the odd goings-on.

Meanwhile, however, her maid – Ann Robinson – had remained at Mr Gresham's to help clear up the mess. While she was there, 'a jar of pickles that stood upon a table, turned upside down, then a jar of rasberry [sic] jam broke to pieces, next two mahogany waiters and a quadrille-box likewise broke in pieces.' It seemed that the ghost was far from finished.

The Stockwell Ghost: '… things in different places began to tumble about, some of them breaking, attended with violent noises all over the house'. (© Anthony Wallis: www.ant-wallis-illustration.blogspot.co.uk.)

Mrs Golding, accompanied by Ann, was taken to stay at her niece's house in Brixton. Her afternoon there passed without incident and Ann was sent back to Stockwell to ask if further disturbances had been reported in their absence. When Ann eventually returned to Brixton she reported that all had been quiet since their departure.

Soon after the maid's return, however, the mysterious destructive power set to work inside the Brixton house. At around 8 p.m.:

… a whole row of pewter dishes, except one, fell from off a shelf to the middle of the floor, rolled about a little while, then settled, [and] as soon as they were quiet, turned upside down; they were then put on the dresser, and went through the same a second time:

next fell a whole row of pewter plates from off the second shelf over the dresser to the ground, and being taken up and put on the dresser one in another, they were thrown down again. The next thing was two eggs that were upon one of the pewter shelves, one of them flew off, crossed the kitchen, struck a cat on the head, and then broke to pieces.

More mayhem followed. Mrs Pain's servant, Mary Martin, went to stoke the kitchen fire and as she drew near a pestle and mortar on the chimney shelf jumped onto the floor, followed shortly afterward by candlesticks and other objects. Those glasses and china that had so far escaped damage were moved onto the floor in the hope that this would prevent further destruction, but before long a glass tumbler that had been placed on the ground 'jumped' about 2ft and broke. Another tumbler nearby also jumped but this one did not break – until it jumped again a few hours later. In the parlour, a china bowl jumped from the floor to behind a table 7ft or 8ft away. The bowl did not break and it was put back where it had been, but some time later it shattered.

Still it went on. A mustard pot jumped out of a cupboard and broke. A cup on the table jumped up, flew across the kitchen, and smashed against the dresser. A tumbler containing rum and water on a table in the parlour jumped about 10ft and broke, and then the table collapsed. A case-bottle flew to pieces. A ham hanging beside the kitchen chimney lifted from its hook and fell to the ground, followed a little while later by another ham hanging on the other side of the chimney. Then a flitch of bacon hanging on the same chimney fell down.

The tract records that: 'All the family were eye witnesses to these circumstances, as well as other persons, some of whom were so alarmed and shocked, that they could not bear to stay, and was happy in getting away, though the unhappy family were left in the midst of their distresses. Most of the genteel families around, were continually sending to enquire after them, and whether all was over or not.'

By about this time, some observers were beginning to suspect that the maid, Ann Robinson, had something to do with what was happening. They had noticed that whenever there was activity, Ann 'was walking backwards and forwards, either in the kitchen or parlour, or wherever some of the family happened to be. Nor could they get her to sit down five minutes together, except at one time for about half an hour towards the morning, when the family were at prayers in the parlour; then all was quiet.'

It was also notable that, while all around her was in uproar and confusion, Ann remained remarkably unperturbed by the chaos. How could it be, wondered the narrator of the tract, 'that a girl of about twenty years old (an age when female timidity is too often assisted by superstition) could remain in the midst of such calamitous circumstances (except they proceeded from causes best known to herself) and not be struck with the same terror as every other person was who was present?'

The disturbances continued throughout the night and by around 5 a.m. on Tuesday 7 January, Mrs Golding and her weary companions fled the farmhouse and sought sanctuary at the house of a neighbour named Richard Fowler. Mr Fowler had been asked to visit the farmhouse the night before: he

had arrived at about 10 p.m. but had been too scared to remain long and had left at around 1 a.m. Unfortunately for him, the 'strange destructive circumstances' now came to his own house.

A candlestick and a tin lamp fell to the ground and a basket of coals tipped over, spilling coal across the floor. Ann Robinson pleaded with Mr Fowler not to let Mrs Golding remain at his house because 'wherever she was, the same things would follow'. Mr Fowler took the maid's advice and, 'fearing greater losses to himself, he desired [Mrs Golding] would quit his house; but first begged her to consider within herself, for her own and public sake, whether or not she had not been guilty of some atrocious crime, for which providence was determined to pursue her'.

Mrs Golding returned to her home at Stockwell, accompanied by her maid and Mr Pain. Soon after they arrived, the mayhem began once more: a 'nine gallon cask of beer, that was in the cellar, the door being open, and no person near it, turned upside down'; a 'pail of water that stood on the floor, boiled like a pot'; a 'box of candles fell from a shelf in the kitchen to the floor, they rolled out, but none were broke' and a 'round mahogany table overset in the parlour.'

Suspicions that Ann was behind the chaos were gathering weight. Mr Pain asked Mrs Golding to send Ann to Brixton to fetch his wife. While the maid was gone, all was quiet. When Ann returned, she was 'immediately discharged' and as the tract's narrator pointedly commented, 'no disturbances have happened since.'

The tract was dated 11 January 1772 and was signed by Mary Golding, John Pain, Mary Pain, Richard Fowler,

Sarah Fowler, and Mary Martin. It records just how much damage was caused during that Monday and Tuesday: 'At Mrs Golding's were broke the quantity of three pails full of glass, china, &c. At Mrs Pain's they filled two pails.' The furniture that survived would later attract great interest. The Revd Daniel Lysons recorded that in around 1790, by which time both Mrs Golding and her daughter had died, 'there was an auction at the house ... when the dancing furniture sold at very extravagant prices.'

Long after the events summarised above, the alleged truth behind the Stockwell Ghost was revealed. The suspicions that had fallen upon Ann Robinson seemed to have been justified when she admitted to the Revd Mr Brayfield that she had hoaxed the entire affair. In his *Extraordinary Popular Delusions and the Madness of Crowds*, author Charles Mackay described the maid's scheme and the methods she claimed to have employed:

> Anne [*sic*], it appears was anxious to have a clear house, to carry on an intrigue with her lover, and she resorted to this trick in order to effect her purpose. She placed the china on the shelves in such a manner that it fell on the slightest motion, and attached horse-hairs to other articles, so that she could jerk them down from an adjoining room without being perceived by any one. She was exceedingly dexterous at this sort of work, and would have proved a formidable rival to many a juggler by profession.

A Ghost on the Northern Line

Late at night and in the early hours of the morning, after the familiar stations of the London Underground are closed to the public, much behind-the-scenes work is carried out to keep the ageing system in working order. It can be eerily quiet and lonely when you're down there in those echoing, almost deserted tunnels. Especially if you can't be certain you're truly alone.

In 1984, Paul was training to be a manager on the Underground and as part of his training he was required to

Stockwell station.

Oval station.

South Island Place, SW9: does the ghost of an Underground railway worker haunt the junction that lies beneath this street?

familiarise himself at first hand with the various procedures staff needed to carry out. One of these procedures was 'track walking', which involved walking through the tunnels that run between stations after all the power had been shut off. Paul was to do this alone, with only his torch to illuminate the way.

He told the story of what happened next in a 2005 television documentary entitled *Ghosts on the Underground*.

He left Oval station and made his way south through the dark Northern Line tunnel, heading towards Stockwell. Several minutes into his journey he came across what he described as a sort of 'clearing', an area where the tunnel widened. There was a man working there.

The man was older than him – perhaps in his fifties – and Paul was a little surprised by the lamp the man was carrying. It was not a modern electric torch, but rather an old-fashioned paraffin-fuelled device known as a Tilley Lamp. These had once been in common use on the London Underground, but by 1984 they had become all but obsolete.

'I'm surprised you've got one of those old lamps,' he commented, to which the man replied that he preferred them to the newer devices. Thinking no more of it, Paul asked the older man where exactly they were and was informed that this was 'South Island Place'.

South Island Place on the Northern Line is a step-plate junction – a junction where tunnels of different diameters join – and it lies beneath the road of the same name, not quite halfway between Oval and Stockwell stations.

After their brief conversation, Paul left the man working and continued to trudge alone through the tunnel to Stockwell.

Having reached his destination, he telephoned the station supervisor at Oval to report that the track had been in good order, and that he was now clear of it. In passing, he asked the supervisor what the other man was doing up at South Island Place, casually dropping the name to show off his newly acquired knowledge.

'What other guy?' replied the supervisor.

Paul explained, but the station supervisor was quite certain that nobody was booked to work down there that night. The two men were left with no option but to go back into the tunnel to search for the mysterious worker.

Paul set off from Stockwell, retracing his journey north through the darkness, while the supervisor reluctantly set off south from Oval. After about twenty minutes the two men met in around the middle of the tunnel. Neither had found any sign of the man with his old-fashioned lamp.

The search wasted a great deal of valuable time, with knock-on delays that meant the first trains of the day had to be held up. Unsurprisingly, Paul's colleagues were less than pleased. What was worse, though, was the angry interview he later had with his trainer, who demanded to know why the trains had been delayed.

Paul related what had happened, and his trainer gave him what he described as 'a very old-fashioned look'.

'You know about South Island Place and the ghost stories, do you?' asked the trainer suspiciously.

When Paul denied any knowledge of such tales, his trainer told him there was a myth that a man had been hit by a train and killed many years before, and that his ghost was supposed to wander those tunnels. It was clear, though, that the trainer believed Paul to be playing some sort of practical joke on him, and that he did not appreciate the humour in the slightest.

According to the 2005 documentary, a maintenance worker had indeed been killed on the Northern Line during the 1950s. He had been working on a noisy compressor and probably hadn't heard the train approaching him.

The driver of that train later reported that the man he hit had been carrying a Tilley Lamp.

6

AROUND STREATHAM

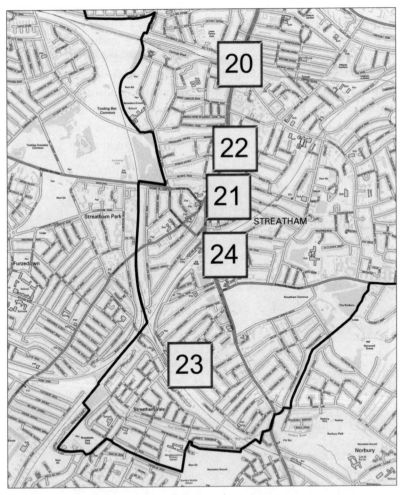

AROUND STREATHAM. *Key: (20) The Many Ghosts of Caesars Nightclub; (21) The Haunted House of Shrubbery Road; (22) The Phantom of the Cinema; (23) A Mysterious Light in Tankerville Road; (24) The Phantom Nun of Coventry Hall. (Contains Ordnance Survey data © Crown copyright and database right 2012.)*

The Many Ghosts of Caesars Nightclub

In 2003 the television series *Most Haunted* filmed an investigation at the Clock House, Surrey Hills, home of a gentleman named Fred Batt. Towards the end of that episode, the show's spiritualist medium, Derek Acorah, declared that he had sensed the presence of a female spirit. He said that the spirit was not actually attached to that building but had instead followed Batt there.

Apparently, this spirit had very light-coloured hair that reminded Acorah of Marilyn Monroe's platinum blonde hairstyle. Furthermore, the medium had picked up the name 'Ruth'. In response, Batt revealed that he owned a nightclub and that among the many people who had worked in that building had been none other than Ruth Ellis – the last woman to be executed for a crime in the United Kingdom.

Batt told the *Most Haunted* team that there had been reports from his club of a blonde woman walking through fire-exit doors, a woman whose ghostly status was evidenced by the fact that the fire doors remained closed as she passed through them. Unsurprisingly, the team decided they should look further into Batt's club and their investigation was duly featured in the show's following episode. The club in question was Caesars in Streatham.

Caesars stood at Nos 156-160 Streatham Hill, where it was hard to miss. Dramatically positioned above the main entrance were the enormous figures of a Roman charioteer and four horses, a decoration in keeping with the Roman

Caesars nightclub, Streatham Hill (photographed here in June 2009) was apparently haunted by a multitude of ghosts. Note the banner advertising The Paranormal Channel on Sky television.

theme used throughout this latest incarnation of the building. The building had originally opened on Tuesday, 1 October 1929. On that date the opening ceremony was carried out by the popular actress Dorothy Seacombe and, as the orchestra struck up a tune and couples took to the floor, what was then the Locarno dance hall sparkled into life.

It developed into one of London's premier dance venues, and among the many stars who appeared at the Locarno during its early years were Charlie Chaplin, Laurel and Hardy, and Glen Miller. By the 1960s it was bands such as The Rolling Stones and The Small Faces, but by that decade the Locarno had also become infamous as a favourite haunt of the London underworld.

As time continued to pass, the Locarno's fortunes faded and the building subsequently went through several further incarnations: 1970 saw the gala opening of the Cat's Whiskers; 1984 the club's re-launch as The Studio; and 1990 another re-launch as The Ritzy. Then, in 1994, Fred Batt took over the building and turned it into Caesars.

It swiftly became a popular and noisy venue, with many and varied attractions on offer over the years, including: disco nights; boxing matches (the first professional female boxing bout took place there in November 1998); cage fighting; and what was advertised as the 'first male lap-dancing club for ladies only'. As well as such boisterous entertainments, however, Caesars apparently had a stranger side: *Most Haunted* introduced it as 'a nightclub … so terrifying that the owner and staff go home with the crowds [because] they are too petrified to stay.' The building was rumoured to be haunted.

The Ghost of Reggie Kray

When the medium Derek Acorah visited Caesars with a television crew he was straight away drawn to an area beside the fire exit on the nightclub's first floor. Almost immediately, Acorah said he sensed the spirit of a man here who was laughing because he knew he wasn't supposed to be there. Acorah said he was picking up a particular phrase: 'Richardson'd go ballistic if he knew I was here. If he knew I was here he'd go ballistic!'

As Acorah explained that this laughing spirit was very close, he abruptly claimed to recognise its identity: it was the notorious London gangster Reginald Kray.

During the 1950s and '60s Reginald 'Reggie' Kray and his brother Ronald – known as 'Ron' or 'Ronnie' – had headed the most feared organised crime gang in London's East End. Protection rackets, armed robberies, arson, torture and murders earned the brothers a reputation for violence, and a sort of dark celebrity status that was bolstered by the glitzy nightclub netherworld in which they moved.

Batt felt that 'Richardson' probably referred to Charlie Richardson of the Richardson Gang of south London criminals, stating that Charlie had indeed visited the club. In the mid-1960s the Richardson Gang had been involved in a vicious turf war with the Krays and the club had been considered to lie within the Richardsons' territory. Despite this, according to the programme, 'Rumour has it that the Krays may have visited the club once or twice.' It was this trespass that was apparently a source of continuing amusement to Reggie Kray's spirit.

The Ghost of Ruth Ellis

Acorah then picked up a second 'energy' in the area beside the fire-exit door, a spiritual presence connected with a pretty, petite woman with virtually white hair. With conviction, Acorah announced that this was Ruth Ellis, adding that she was familiarly calling him 'Derek' and had commented that she liked his 'sharp' suit!

Batt confirmed that staff at Caesars had reportedly seen the ghost of a young blonde-haired woman wearing old-fashioned clothes standing beside that same fire exit, and then turning and walking through the closed doors. As he had stated in the previous episode, the apparition was believed to be that of Ellis. Batt told the team that every time he visited this particular area of the club he felt his hair stand on end.

Ruth Neilson (later Ellis) was born in Rhyl, North Wales, on 9 October 1926. There she spent the first few years of her childhood, but with the UK economy in a poor state and unemployment on the rise, her family was among the many who migrated south in search of a better life. Ruth hated being poor and as she grew up she developed a driving ambition to make something of herself. She was determined that the world would take notice of her.

The world, meanwhile, set about tearing itself apart. In the aftermath of the Blitz (September 1940 to May 1941) London had been left reeling by the German Luftwaffe, but a fierce vitality was burning within many of the occupants of the bomb-pounded city, a determination to live for today because tomorrow might never come. It was a hedonistic spirit that Ruth could wholeheartedly embrace, and the city irresistibly called to her.

Her looks had blossomed, and so had her sexuality. There is little doubt that Ruth became sexually active at an early age, and with her hair bleached a dramatic peroxide blonde and her personality seemingly unfettered by any inhibitions, the 5ft 2in teenager easily found the recognition she craved flaunting herself on the floor of the Locarno dance hall.

She found work there too, becoming, for a time, the personal assistant to the Locarno's in-house photographer. That job gave the young Ruth access to some of the Locarno's wealthiest and most important clients, as well as a taste for their glamorous lifestyle.

The Locarno would prove important in another way too, for it was here that she found the first great love of her life. During the Second World War the club was a favourite haunt of servicemen on leave. Most were Americans and Canadians far from home and with plenty of money to spend, and Ruth encouraged more than one of them to fall for her charms. At the age of seventeen (in 1943 or 1944), she unexpectedly fell in love with a French-Canadian soldier named Clare (his surname is not known).

Ruth became pregnant, and Clare proposed marriage. The story might have turned out well had it not transpired that Clare already had a wife and children back in Canada. He sailed home on a troopship and sent Ruth money for a few months before breaking off contact. Ruth never heard from him again. On 15 September 1944 she gave birth to his son.

Now she had a child to support. After getting her figure back, Ruth answered an advert in a local newspaper and ended up striking 'artistic nude poses' for members of a Camera Club. The nude modelling led her into working for Morris 'Maurie'

Conley (memorably described in *The People* newspaper as 'Britain's biggest vice-boss') as a hostess in his drinking clubs, and there she supplemented her income with occasional prostitution. Before long she became pregnant by one of her clients – who quickly vanished after she told him – and visited a private clinic for the first of several abortions.

In 1950 (not long after another abortion), twenty-four-year-old Ruth met forty-one-year-old George Ellis, a divorced, heavy-drinking dentist who was a regular client of Conley's Court Club. They married later that same year but the marriage soon broke down. George had become wholly dependent on drink and, under its influence, could become violent towards Ruth. For her part, Ruth's own increasingly heavy drinking was making it harder to rein in the jealousy to which she was all too prone. By the time their daughter was born in October 1951 their marriage was over in all but name. George left her.

Her daughter's birth had been difficult, and Ruth recovered only slowly, but eventually she returned to work as a hostess for Conley. By now the privations of a post-war economy were dissipating, and London's West End clubs were enjoying a boom period. The Court Club had moved up-market and changed its name to Carroll's. It was doing well for itself, as was another of Conley's enterprises – the Little Club in Knightsbridge, west London …

As the *Most Haunted* cameras continued filming, Derek Acorah made an announcement. Ruth Ellis had apparently told him: 'David's here with me […] We've found our love again.' The programme's host, Yvette Fielding, turned to Fred Batt to ask if he knew

who this 'David' might be, but Acorah hadn't finished. He and Batt replied simultaneously: 'David Blakely'.

David Blakely was a young, handsome and hard-drinking racing driver from a well-to-do public-school background. He first encountered Ruth Ellis in Carroll's in around September or October of 1953, during one of his many rowdy drinking sessions with fellow racing car drivers and their entourages. Ruth, for once, was not there for work but had gone along as a guest of some of the members.

Drunkenly, Blakely voiced some derogatory – and probably offensively sexual – remarks about the club's hostesses, irritating the brassy blonde who overheard him. 'Who is that pompous little ass?' she loudly asked her companions. It was an inauspicious start to their relationship.

At around this same time, Conley made Ruth manager of the Little Club. She would later claim that the first customer she ever served there turned out to be Blakely. Despite their disastrous first meeting, the couple were sleeping together within a fortnight. Theirs would be a passionate love affair, but one that was doomed from the outset.

Even if tough little Ruth could ever have been accepted by Blakely's higher-class social set, the peroxide blonde was by now heavily reliant on alcohol to keep up the effervescent exterior necessary for her job. One effect of her drinking was to bring dangerously close to the surface the violent jealousy that had already been evidenced in her relationship with George Ellis.

The lovers argued frequently and hotly as their self-destructive relationship spiralled out of control. The arguments were fuelled by heavy drinking on both their parts. The huge bar tab Blakely ran up at the Little Club – a tab he had no real intention of paying back – was part of the reason Ruth lost her job there at the end of 1954. Early the following year she discovered she was pregnant again, but she could not be sure who the father was. (Both she and Blakely slept with other people on various occasions throughout their time together.) In early 1955 she suffered a miscarriage, later claiming that it had been brought on by one of her many physical fights with Blakely, during which he had punched her in the stomach.

Things came to a climax in April 1955. Blakely had been due to race his beloved car, 'The Emperor', but was forced to pull out after it broke down during a practice lap. Furious, he blamed the fault on Ruth, calling her a jinx. On Friday 8 April, the beginning of the Easter Bank Holiday weekend, Blakely went to visit his friend and chief mechanic, Anthony 'Ant' Findlater, to discuss what could be done with 'The Emperor'. The Findlaters later stated that Blakely and Ruth had had a furious argument before he left, something Ruth denied.

Ruth was seething with jealousy. She suspected that Blakely was having an affair, and there was no love lost between Ruth and the Findlaters, especially as she knew that Blakely had at one time also had an affair with Ant's wife, Carole.

Late that evening, Blakely had not come home. Ruth started to telephone the Findlaters, demanding to speak to her lover. On her second call, Ant told her Blakely was not there, but Ruth was convinced otherwise.

She grew increasingly frantic, becoming certain that the Findlaters were trying to persuade Blakely to desert her. By the early hours of the morning she was hysterical. She persuaded Desmond Cussen (another of her lovers) to drive her to the Findlaters' second-floor flat at No. 29 Tanza Road, in Hampstead, north London, where she hammered on the door. When there was no answer she vented her rage on Blakely's car, which she found parked in the road outside.

Blakely was indeed in the flat, having met Ant and Carole at the Magdala pub in South Hill Park, Hampstead, for lunchtime drinks on Friday. He had told the Findlaters that he wanted to get away from Ruth Ellis, prophetically telling Carole, 'You don't know her. You don't know what she can do.'

Blakely refused to go downstairs to meet the screaming woman. The police were called and eventually Cussen persuaded Ruth to let him drive her away. Blakely stayed at the Findlaters' flat.

Ruth spent Saturday travelling back and forth between her home and Tanza Road, alternately brooding – convincing herself that Blakely was having an affair with the Findlaters' young nanny – and exploding into rage, growing ever more frenzied as the twin passions of love and hatred fought within her for control. Another sleepless night left her bitter and wanting revenge, and on the morning of Easter Sunday (10 April) she telephoned the Findlaters again. Ant answered.

'I hope you are having an enjoyable holiday,' said Ruth, 'because you have ruined mine.'

Ant hung up.

At her trial, Ruth would state that she could not recall how she spent most of that Sunday.

Blakely, meanwhile, was badly hungover, as were the Findlaters.

That lunchtime the three of them went to the Magdala for a 'hair of the dog', where they met a friend, Clive Gunnell, and invited him to visit the Tanza Road flat for a drink that evening. In the afternoon, Blakely and the Findlaters visited the Easter fairground on Hampstead Heath.

Ellis spent the afternoon and evening with Cussen. She had gone without sleep for three days now, sustained by nicotine, emotional turmoil, and a mind-twisting cocktail of prescription tranquilisers and Pernod.

Blakely and his friends passed the evening at the flat, drinking, smoking, listening to music, and no doubt discussing what should be done about his crazy lover. At around 8.45 p.m., they ran out of cigarettes. Blakely offered to fetch some more from the Magdala and Gunnell went with him. As the two men drove away they were seen by Ruth.

She had again travelled to Hampstead and she correctly guessed where their car was headed. She made her own way to the Magdala, where she found Blakely's car parked.

At around 9.30 p.m., Blakely and Gunnell came out of the pub.

'Hello, David,' said Ruth.

He ignored her, walking to his car.

She shouted after him: 'David!'

Blakely rummaged for his car keys. Ruth reached into her handbag, took out a .38 calibre Smith & Wesson revolver, and fired at him.

Her first shot missed. Blakely started to run but was caught by her second shot. She stood over him, continuing to fire as he lay on the ground. In total she shot him four times, once from so close a range that it left powder burns on his skin.

Ruth had a final bullet left in the revolver and eye-witness reports suggest that she attempted to take her own life but either the gun jammed or she lost her nerve. Standing over Blakely's dying body, seemingly mesmerised by what she had done, she lowered the gun – and now it fired for the last time. The bullet ricocheted from the road, slightly injuring a bystander.

Ruth appeared to be in a state of shock as she asked Gunnell to fetch the police, and she put up no resistance as she was arrested. As the still-smoking gun was taken from her, she told the policeman, 'I am guilty. I'm a little confused.' She was taken to Hampstead police station, where she made a full confession and was charged with murder.

On Monday 20 June 1955 Ruth Ellis appeared before Mr Justice Havers in the Number One Court at the Old Bailey.

'When you fired the revolver at close range into the body of David Blakely, what did you intend to do?' asked the prosecution.

'It's obvious when I shot him I intended to kill him,' Ruth replied.

Her response and the appearance she deliberately presented (against her counsel's advice) of a tough brassy blonde guaranteed a guilty verdict, and the mandatory sentence of death. The jury took less than a quarter of an hour to confirm that guilt and after receiving sentence Ruth was taken to the condemned cell at Holloway prison.

From that cell she wrote a final letter to Blakely's parents, telling them: 'I have always loved your son, and I shall die still loving him.'

Just before 9 a.m. on Wednesday, 13 July 1955, the hangman Albert Pierrepoint and his assistant escorted twenty-eight-year-old Ruth from her cell to the execution room next door.

Seconds later she was hanging dead at the end of a rope.

It was the ending she had believed she deserved, considering it fit justice for killing the man she had loved. Nevertheless, the case caused widespread public controversy and national soul searching over the right of the Crown to execute, and it helped to harden public opinion over the death penalty. Ruth Ellis would be the last female to receive that penalty. Over the following years it became increasingly common for reprieves to be granted, and the last UK execution of a man was carried out less than a decade later, in 1964.

Despite her confession, there are those who believe that Ruth did not personally fire the final, killing shot. They point the finger at her 'alternative lover', Desmond Cussen. It was probably this theory that was being alluded to when Derek Acorah told the *Most Haunted* team that Ellis's spirit kept repeating to him that 'they' hadn't got it right, that she had fired the gun only three times rather than four as had been reported. She knew the number, she said (via Acorah) because she had fired the gun, 'and David knew as well.'

Later, Acorah added that Ruth Ellis's spirit was now ready to go away to her 'rightful place' with David Blakely and would only return to visit the club periodically.

However, fortunately for the *Most Haunted* team the nightclub seemed to have plenty of other ghosts that might yet make their presence known …

Ghosts of the Ground Floor

Among the other areas of Caesars that had become associated with strange happenings was the dance floor on the building's ground floor. This was where the terrifying sound of a woman screaming had supposedly been heard on numerous occasions.

Behind the dance floor was an area housing a corridor and two dressing rooms within a separate, low, flat-roofed building that joined onto the main building.

Fred Batt explained that this area had been unused since around the late 1940s. The rooms had been bricked up, but he had had them re-opened and refurbished. Since then members of staff had felt cold spots, experienced feelings of being watched, and seen the doors opening and closing on their own. The atmosphere in the dressing rooms was said to be oppressive and the sound of footsteps had been heard in the empty corridor.

Acorah felt that Batt's reopening of the bricked-up backstage area had reactivated the 'residual energy' there, allowing it to surge out of the rooms and into the corridor.

The medium sensed a connection between the dressing rooms and two men, both since deceased, and a female accomplice, who had practised 'the Black Arts' here in around the 1940s. It was 'the living energy of thought' from these two men that had become trapped in this area. He felt that the two men and their female accomplice had all been well-known public figures, although he either couldn't or wouldn't reveal their names, saying that it would not have been the responsible thing to do.

While filming in these dressing rooms, the *Most Haunted* team heard thumping and dragging noises coming from overhead. When told that there were no rooms above them, only the flat roof, they headed to the roof to look for evidence of who (or what) could possibly be making the sounds. The doors leading up to the roof proved to be locked, and after unlocking these and venturing to the roof they found it completely empty.

To the present author, the sounds were very similar to those made by squirrels, gulls, and crows as they stomp around on my own home's flat roof. Acorah, on the other hand, felt confident that they had been a supernatural manifestation.

The First Floor's Haunted Corridor
Another apparently haunted area within the club was a corridor on the first floor, a corridor given an eerily anachronistic atmosphere by its decor, which had remained unchanged since the 1940s.

Here Acorah sensed the spirit of a young girl aged somewhere between five and nine years old. She had very short hair worn with a clip and wore a floral patterned frock, and the medium felt that she had died somewhere close by this corridor.

He had the impression that she had rushed past, and even through, living people – probably members of staff – there, and that she might have been glimpsed as a shadow or felt as a cool rush of air, combined with the feeling of someone 'walking over your grave'. She made very loud noises at times while running, said Acorah, going on to widen this by suggesting that she moved about and may have appeared elsewhere in the club too.

While not exactly confirming Acorah's impressions, Batt did say that this particular area of the club had been used as a crèche from the 1920s through to the 1950s. Since then the corridor hadn't really been used, so it was perhaps

unlikely that anyone would have seen the girl's spirit there.

Acorah went on to say that the girl had probably not been murdered but had instead had an accident somewhere very close to this corridor, possibly a fall onto something in which she had badly hurt herself in the centre of her forehead.

Batt stated that there was some 'evidence' of the doors in that corridor opening on their own (which seems to imply that the doors had been found in an open state rather than actually been seen to move). Acorah confirmed that it was the little girl's spirit that had opened them.

When Batt reminded the team of the reported sound of screaming from the dance floor, Acorah stated that this was unconnected with the little girl's spirit, but was instead to do with yet another ghost attached to the building. This spirit was female too, he felt, but older, perhaps aged around eighteen, and had lost her life 'in an unnatural way', possibly by being strangled. He sensed that she had been pulled along the corridor. Suddenly he picked up on the name Kate or Katie McIntyre, but the *Most Haunted* team was subsequently unable to find any records of a person by that name having a connection with the building.

Acorah believed that Kate/Katie had been a prostitute. She had not expected the man to turn violent, he felt; in fact, he might not have intended to kill her at all. Acorah suggested that the dragging noises the team had heard while in the dressing rooms downstairs might have been a re-enactment of the sound of her body being pulled along this corridor by her ankles. After rendering her unconscious, the attacker had tried to drag her somewhere but she had recovered consciousness and screamed.

To stop her cries he had knelt down and strangled her.

'Orbs' in the Basement

Despite the numerous ghostly phenomena reported, the many impressions received by Derek Acorah, and their own expectant hopes, the *Most Haunted* team experienced little of note during the vigils they held in various parts of the building later that night. The night was not wholly without incident, however.

At around 2.45 a.m. Karl Beattie, the show's director and producer, took two night-vision cameras to the No. 3 dressing room, which was located in the basement beneath the other two dressing rooms.

At 3.10 a.m. he asked aloud for Ruth Ellis to try to manifest herself to him in the form of 'a mist or an orb' at the top of the stairs that led back up to the ground floor. A moment later, one of his cameras picked up a 'light anomaly' or 'orb' about halfway up the stairs. After several further calls for Ruth to make her presence known, a second 'orb' was recorded.

'Orbs' are those circles of light that sometimes appear in photographs and on film. They started to become common with the commercial availability of early digital cameras in the 1990s and, largely as a result of digital photographs being taken in less than ideal conditions inside dim, dusty, and reputedly haunted locations, the idea developed that 'orbs' were a paranormal phenomenon. Today, although the association of 'orbs' with the paranormal remains popular with the media, most serious researchers consider 'orbs' to be nothing more than photographic artefacts.

That said, according to the programme the only two occasions during the entire investigation on which any of these 'light anomalies' were picked up by the cameras happened to be at the very same times that Karl was calling for Ruth to show herself. As the show's parapsychology expert – Ciarán O'Keeffe – asked viewers, was this just coincidence or was there some significance in this?

A Pinch of Salt

The *Most Haunted* episode looking at Caesars was an interesting and enjoyable piece of television, but there are reasons for approaching its findings with caution.

Unusually for the show, Derek Acorah had prior knowledge of the location they were going to visit, which must make it suspicious that the information he produced regarding the presence of Ruth Ellis's spirit was remarkably specific – more so than he usually offered. He was, for example, able to give David Blakely's full name as opposed to his usual ability to supply only a first name (a limitation that frequently hampered the *Most Haunted* researchers' attempts to find historical verification of his impressions). This inevitably casts some doubt over how far to trust what he claimed during his visit to Caesars, especially given that Ciarán O'Keeffe, the aforementioned parapsychologist, later announced that he had caught Acorah cheating on several occasions during the filming of other episodes, pretending to communicate with spirits while actually repeating information he had acquired beforehand.

Quite how much faith should be placed in the claims of a programme that was, after all, intended as entertainment is debatable. But inevitably, the *Most Haunted* investigation will always now be a major part of the story of Caesars nightclub and its ghosts.

It is worth remembering, however, that even if all of Acorah's statements are discounted, something remains. According to Fred Batt there had been reports of strange phenomena at Caesars long before Acorah and the rest of the *Most Haunted* team ever became involved.

Friday, 13 February 2009: The Final Investigation

By the beginning of 2009, the end was in sight for Caesars. The nightclub had been earmarked for demolition, with the site being destined for a major residential and retail development.

Fred Batt was still the owner, and in January 2009 he invited various teams of paranormal investigators from across the UK to visit the premises for a final investigation scheduled to start at 8 p.m. on the spookily significant date of Friday 13

February, and going on until 4 a.m. on the Saturday morning. Members of the public were invited to take part, with tickets for the event going on sale at £45 each.

Publicity for the ghost hunt advertised the belief that ghosts haunting the building included the spirits of Ruth Ellis and 'the Kray twins'. (By now, Reggie Kray had apparently been joined by his brother Ronnie.)

One of the groups involved in the final investigation was the Cleveland Paranormal Investigators (C.P.I.) from the north-east of England. Their leader, Trevor Weller, was confident that it would be an eventful occasion, stating beforehand that 'whenever a building is about to be knocked down paranormal activity increases.'

Weller told *Streatham Guardian* reporter Matt Watts that 85 per cent

As at mid-2012, Caesars nightclub was still awaiting demolition, although the iconic Roman charioteer had been removed.

of people who attended the group's investigations have some kind of paranormal experience, and invited him along to see for himself.

Watts did attend the event, and wrote about it afterwards in an article dated 17 February. Also attending were plenty of others who had bought tickets in the hope of experiencing contact with the otherworldly.

Among the investigators was full-time psychic medium Dr Marty Cia. Only five minutes into the event, reported Watts, Cia told him that he had already made contact with a spirit named Ruth, adding that someone had suggested to him that this might be the spirit of Ruth Ellis. Sceptically, Watts asked if the medium had carried out any background research into the club's suspected hauntings beforehand. Cia assured him this was not the case.

For the next few hours, Watts and the paying members of the public explored the club in groups led by the more seasoned investigators. They participated in vigils, in which everyone sat quietly in the dark in the hope that something would happen, and at other times in seances intended to establish contact with the spirits. At one point Watts took part in a Ouija board session but his group experienced less success than another whose four members believed they successfully contacted the spirit of a former barmaid who had supposedly been strangled to death inside the club. (Whether any historical evidence was found to back this claim up was not reported.)

During another (or possibly the same) Ouija board session, a woman believed she caught the scent of rosewater perfume, and when she smelled the same scent a short while afterwards she was so frightened she fainted.

The paranormal investigators had brought with them various technical gadgets and from time to time their equipment created some excitement. A number of 'orbs' appeared in photographs taken during the event and on one occasion, reported Watts, a thermometer recorded a drop in temperature within a room as Dr Cia was apparently communicating with the spirit of Ruth Ellis. (The number of degrees was not given.)

'The investigators are clearly buoyed by their findings and seem in no doubt that the club is haunted,' concluded Watts, but he was obviously left less than convinced by the whole experience.

The Death of Caesars

Caesars nightclub closed its doors for the last time in 2010, but Fred Batt's association with the supernatural – and with *Most Haunted* – did not end with the demise of his haunted nightclub. As of December 2011, he describes himself as a 'Demonologist and Master of the Dark Arts' on his website (www.fredbatt.com), and he has been credited as a 'demonologist' on *Most Haunted Live!*

The Haunted House of Shrubbery Road

From the police station at the junction with Streatham High Road, Shrubbery Road curves gracefully to the south as it descends a gentle incline. It feels like a relatively peaceful place, but in March 1984 a short article in the *South Western Star* newspaper reported that a particular

Shrubbery Road in Streatham, where a house was reportedly haunted for several decades.

(unidentified) house in this road had been plagued by mysterious happenings for the previous thirty years.

The house had been home to the same family since the 1950s. From the outside it had seemed no different to any of its neighbours, yet uncanny events started to occur there almost as soon as the family moved in. Pots and pans would, for no apparent reason, fall from their usual places on the scullery shelf and crash to the floor. The scullery was also where the apparition of a 'gentleman dressed all in black with a cloak and hat' was seen 'quite often'.

Another apparition sometimes manifested in the bedrooms. This was of an old lady attired in the clothing of a child's nanny. 'The nanny', as it was referred to, was seen on many occasions by Kay, the mother of the family, who told how she would sometimes awake during the night to find the spectre gazing down at her. 'Often,' said Kay, 'all you would see was just her eyes staring.'

According to Kay, her son had also seen the nanny several times while he was a toddler. One night, the young lad began choking because, she believed, the fear induced by 'seeing these two eyes had made his throat constrict'. After this worrying incident it seemed that the nanny ceased to watch over the family at night, although they still caught the occasional glimpse of the apparition drifting through the bedrooms.

Even the family's pet cat acted oddly at times, they felt, as if watching invisible beings moving around the house (although readers familiar with the sometimes peculiar behaviour of cats might wonder whether there was anything truly unusual in this).

Of all the strange occurrences, the most frightening was when Kay awoke one night to discover a 'swirling gas' forming around her bed. 'It seemed really malevolent,' she recalled, and she was so scared that, despite not being religious, she resorted to the Lord's Prayer, reciting it over and over until at last the eerie mist dissipated.

Eventually the family arranged to have a medium exorcise the house and this seemed to help, removing the sense of brooding evil they had long felt hung over the building. Yet the exorcism did not mark the end of the story.

The most recent event recorded in the article happened shortly before Christmas 1983 when 'gritty, rust-coloured water' started to drip from the ceiling by the staircase. Kay looked to see where it was coming from and, as she did so, 'clear pure water began cascading down the stairs'. Within minutes, however, the water had disappeared and both stairs and floor were completely dry. She did not discover where the water had come from and, presumably, the mysterious leak had not repeated itself in the two-and-a-half months between then and the newspaper article.

Seeking to understand why the house should be haunted, Kay looked into its history and reportedly discovered that a mortuary had once stood on land behind the property. The house had also apparently been the site of a suicide and the sudden death of an infant, and Kay felt that this latter tragedy might explain the apparition of the nanny. She speculated that what she had seen was the spirit of the dead child's nanny and that it had meant no harm, seeking only to atone for a previous failure by protectively watching over Kay's young son.

The Phantom of the Cinema

The birth of Streatham's Odeon cinema was a glorious affair.

On 30 June 1930 more than 2,500 people attended the opening night of what was then the Astoria. They had ostensibly arrived for the screening of the musical comedy *Paris*, but they had also come to marvel at the building itself. Standing at the junction of Streatham High Road and Pendennis Road, and designed by the architect E.A. Stone, the cinema's magnificent interior was modelled on an Ancient Egyptian theme, with dramatic red, green and gold paintwork enhanced by cleverly concealed lighting, and Egyptian-styled bas-reliefs decorating the circle walls.

It was all highly glamorous and it gave the building a frisson of thrilling mysticism, evoking a sense of Ancient Egypt's mystery and magic. But the uncanny event that occurred at the Astoria a few short years after that opening night seemed related not to distant Egypt but rather to the very ground on which the cinema had been built.

It happened on Christmas night, 1933. Lewis Amis, the Astoria's fireman, was patrolling the empty cinema and undoubtedly looking forward to returning to the warmth of his home and family. Shining his torch into the gloomy shadows around him, he walked into the darkened tea lounge – and as he did so he was shocked to see a figure moving towards him.

His first thought was that he had disturbed a burglar. He turned his torch directly into the face of the figure, and its light revealed an elderly man dressed in a long white gown. The gown's hood was pulled up, and the figure's arms hung stiffly at its sides as it drew closer to Amis, seeming to glide across the floor. As it neared, Amis caught sight of the face beneath the hood, describing this to a *Daily Mail* reporter two days later as 'a wizened, wrinkled face [with] a short beard'.

Then the figure turned away from him, moving towards a flight of stairs that led down to the vestibule. Nervous, and uncertain as to whether he had encountered a phantom or a mortal intruder, Amis followed it downstairs towards the large wooden fire doors that led through to the stalls.

As Amis explained to the reporter, these doors were 'heavy, strongly fastened, and three men would have a job to get them open.' Yet, as the figure neared them, the doors swung apart.

Amis followed the figure as it passed through the open doorway and down the centre aisle of the auditorium, and he watched in disbelief as it then 'leapt, or rather floated, across the orchestra pit, landing behind the footlights in front of the curtain.'

All at once, the apparition turned to face the now terrified fireman. It raised its arms and, in a 'weird, husky voice', cried out: 'I won't sell, I won't sell, I won't sell!'

With that, it vanished, and Amis was once again alone.

Lewis Amis was not someone who particularly believed in the supernatural; the newspaper described him as 'a hard-headed citizen of Clapham'. He seemed to be telling the truth, but had the fireman been the unwitting victim of a bizarre prank, or had he really seen a ghost?

News of the incident was brought (probably by the journalist who took down Amis's story) to the widow of a man named Alfred Frederick Janes. Amis

The Odeon cinema, Streatham. Built on the site of Chesterfield House, the building originally opened in 1930 as the Astoria.

had never heard of Alfred Janes but if he had known of him he would surely have suspected it was that man's ghost he had seen, for the Astoria cinema had been built on the site of Janes's old home – a home he had been most reluctant to sell.

In around 1901 Alfred Janes and his family had moved into a large Victorian property called Chesterfield House, which stood surrounded by large gardens on the ground the Astoria cinema would occupy a few decades later. It was a fine building and many locals regarded the old cherry tree in its front garden with great fondness for the way its cheerfully bedecked branches hung out over Streatham High Road.

Janes loved the building, and so he was highly irritated when, after living there for more than a quarter of a century, he began to be pestered by property developers. They wanted to buy Chesterfield House in order to redevelop the site. He declined their offer. This was his home and he would not sell. They offered more money. He declined again. They made a higher offer, and so it went on, with the developers refusing to admit defeat.

Eventually Janes conceded and, full of misgivings, he agreed to sell Chesterfield House. In 1929 he and his wife moved to a new home in Streatham Common South.

Chesterfield House was pulled down, the cheerful old cherry tree disappeared from Streatham, and in their place gradually rose the mighty new Astoria. Less than a fortnight after the new cinema's grand opening night, Alfred Janes died.

Although the *Daily Mail* reporter seems to have been keen to make a connection between this historical background and the ghost story, it appears that Mr Janes's widow was less than entirely convinced. In answer to the journalist's questions, she simply replied: 'It is true my husband was attached to the house, and it is true he had a beard.'

Despite this rather non-committal answer, the resulting newspaper article's implication was clear: the ghost encountered by Lewis Amis might have been that of Alfred Janes, haunting the site of the beloved family home he had so reluctantly given up.

The hushed, enveloping darkness and flickering shadows inside a cinema can easily give rise to all sorts of misperceptions, but perhaps two more recently reported sightings from within what is now the Odeon Streatham are in some way connected with the building's earlier ghost story.

In November 2011, cinema manager Sussannah Mortimer told me of two strange incidents she had personally experienced during her seventeen years working in this building. Both took place 'in what is now Screen 1 [back] when it was a six-screen cinema.'

In 2001, Sussannah walked through the main entrance to Screen 1 as part of one of her regular checks that all was well in the building. In addition to the few members of the public sitting watching the film, she spotted the shadowy figure of what she took to be one of her security men leaning against the right-hand wall. Walking out, she contacted security to ask who was in there, but was advised that there were no security or any other staff in Screen 1 at that time. When Sussannah returned to Screen 1, the man was no longer there and the audience was still watching the film, unaware of anything untoward.

Around five years later, in 2006, Sussannah saw what she described as 'a thin, tall aristocratic lady in a long white dress, who walked from the bottom left-hand side of the screen, all the way to the top of the screen staircase ... This was while the screen was on, but no one [else was] in [there] at the time.'

As far as Sussannah was aware, however, there had been no further reports of anything resembling the figure seen by Lewis Amis that Christmas night in 1933.

A Mysterious Light in Tankerville Road

Late one night in around 1953, 'John' (pseudonym) was woken by a scream. He later learned that this had been his stepmother starting from a nightmare in her bedroom one floor below.

John was about thirteen years old and for the previous few years had been living in this house in Tankerville Road, Streatham, with his three younger brothers, his father, his stepmother, and his stepmother's mother. He shared a bedroom on the top floor with his brother 'Mike' (pseudonym) who, it appeared, was still asleep.

All was quiet again now. Lying in the darkness, John closed his eyes and waited to drift back into sleep but when he was still awake a few minutes later he blearily lifted his eyelids. That was when he noticed something strange.

On the wall opposite him, approximately 10ft away, was a circular patch of light, roughly the same diameter as a tennis ball and white in the centre, dimming to yellow around the circumference. Its glow was not particularly intense – perhaps as bright as a single candle – but it commanded his attention because there seemed no reason for it to be there.

There were no light sources inside the room and the only small window overlooked a narrow alleyway running between the house and its neighbour, and was covered with a curtain. Even if any light, perhaps from a streetlight or a car outside, could have shone in through that window (and it never had before), the wall on which the patch of light hung was that at the front of the house: the angle was such that the light would almost have had to double back on itself as it came through the window, and there was nothing in the room it could have been reflecting from.

As these thoughts troubled his drowsy mind, John's initial mild interest grew into mounting unease. Was he dreaming? He shut his eyes for a moment then re-opened them. The light was still there, looking just the same as before. Then it began to move.

Very slowly, it slid across the surface of the wall, moving from left to right. It glided down a short distance, possibly edging a little to the left as it did so, then resumed its movement to the right, in the general direction of Mike's bed. Its speed stayed steady – slow and deliberate – and its outline remained perfectly circular.

Tankerville Road, where an inexplicable patch of light terrified a schoolboy in the 1950s.

The patch of light crept ever closer to his brother's bed and as John continued to watch in silence his unease swelled into terror. Suddenly, he could take no more. He screamed for help.

His stepmother came running up to see what was wrong and as she entered she switched on the bedroom light. The mysterious patch on the wall either vanished or was drowned in the glare. It was not seen again.

This odd incident was never spoken of until some forty-five years later when John gave me this account. Shortly afterwards, his stepmother told me that she still remembered that night, and commented that the entire time she had lived in that house she had never liked being in that top-floor bedroom. In particular she had taken a strong dislike to the door that led from that bedroom to the loft area housing the water tank. She was unable to clarify what it was about the door that she disliked – just that it had made her uncomfortable. She had never ascribed any significance to this, and had never told anybody about it. In fact, she only mentioned it at all because she now wondered if her unease had somehow been associated with whatever was behind that mysterious light in the Tankerville Road house.

(N.B.: In 1975 two schoolgirls had a somewhat similar experience in a house in Mitcham; I recount their tale in my *Strange Mitcham*.)

The Phantom Nun of Coventry Hall

Coventry Hall stands in Polworth Road, a short distance to the north of Streatham Common. Although the present building dates back only as far as the end of the twentieth century, the site on which it stands has a far longer and much more interesting history, and the building that previously occupied this spot was said to be haunted by a phantom nun.

That building was also called Coventry Hall, and that itself had been built on the site of an even older structure, the old Streatham Manor House, which had stood here from at least Tudor times. The manor house was purchased in 1798 by George William Coventry (known as Viscount Deerhurst and later to become the 7th Earl of Coventry) and it was he who had the old building pulled down to make way for a fashionable villa.

That villa – the first 'Coventry Hall' – was constructed in the early 1800s. George died in 1831, and by around 1895 Coventry Hall had become a convent. The nuns living there – the Sisters of St Andrew – later established a school in the building, but at the outbreak of the Second World War the school was evacuated to Worthing.

Now the large old building stood, dark, silent and deserted. It was practically inevitable that rumours would start to circulate, telling of the sound of chanting drifting out from inside those abandoned walls, and the lights of candles flickering in the shadows beyond the empty windows. Practically inevitable – but perhaps in this instance the rumours had some substance to them.

As Hitler's Germany punished Londoners for their refusal to capitulate and the war dragged grimly on, a pair of Irishmen – Tom Connelly and James Duggan – trudged back to their lodgings late one night after carrying out bomb-damage repairs somewhere in Wandsworth. It was November 1944, and as Connelly and Duggan walked past Coventry Hall both men heard what they at first took to be the sound of people whispering. Listening more intently, they thought that the noise seemed to become more of a rustling, as of cloth being drawn across the ground.

They looked towards the old convent and saw, no more than 100 yards from them, what seemed to be a group of shadowy cowled figures. It was dark, and difficult to make out the details, but it appeared to be a group of nuns, quietly passing the building, their long habits rustling softly as they dragged across the grass.

When the Second World War finally ended, the school decided not to return to Coventry Hall. Faced with an acute shortage of housing accommodation, the council promptly set about converting the three-storey building into flats.

It should have been a straightforward job, but the workmen charged with making the necessary alterations found their tasks continually interfered with by an unknown pest. On numerous occasions they complained that their tools and materials had disappeared from where they had left them overnight, the missing items later turning up in other parts of the building.

On one particular occasion, the workers left a large number of tools, scaffold boards and ladders in the large room that had once been the convent's chapel. Overnight, every item was moved from that room.

The more down-to-earth of the workmen directed their suspicions towards local boys, who they believed might be breaking into the building at night to cause mischief. Some of their colleagues felt otherwise: would boys playing on the site bother to leave the various tools and other materials in the manner in which these would always be discovered, neatly and carefully stacked rather than simply left lying around?

Despite the unexplained interferences the construction work was eventually completed, and by 1947 Coventry Hall had been converted into thirty-three flats. Families began to move in, but (according to claims made a few years later) some of the new tenants almost immediately felt there was something odd about the building.

During the autumn of 1955, Mrs Evelyn Sayers – a thirty-year-old mother of two – awoke one night feeling cold and overcome with a powerful feeling of melancholy. Something was wrong, she felt, and the sensation was so strong that she left the warmth of her bed to check that her children were okay.

She found them safely asleep, if rather restless, but Evelyn remained unhappy. She walked around the flat, making sure everything was as it should be. Nothing seemed to be out of order, yet still that sense of 'something being wrong' persisted.

Looking around the living room, Evelyn found her attention drawn to the front door. Checking that it was properly shut and locked, she was about to turn away when the idea gripped her that she should open the door immediately, that someone was waiting for her on the other side.

Unable to resist, she took hold of the handle and, as if compelled by some outside force, she drew back the bolt and opened the door. There, standing in the cold night air, was the spectral figure of a nun.

Evelyn tried to scream, but no sound came from her constricted throat.

Riveted to the spot, she could only watch in horrified silence as the nun raised her arm. Despite her terror, Evelyn registered that the gesture was seemingly intended as reassurance.

The nun spoke with a soft voice: 'Do not be afraid. Just say … God … be … with … you …'

Long pauses separated the last words, and as the voice died away Evelyn's trapped scream at last burst forth. Her abruptly awakened neighbours came rushing out of their flats to see what was wrong and found her standing in her doorway, ashen-faced, trembling, and alone.

The next day Evelyn Sayers did the most practical thing she could think of: she wrote to her landlords – the local council – to tell them about the ghost in Coventry Hall. Her letter reached the borough housing manager, Mr L. Dean, who treated the matter seriously and suggested that she contact the Society for Psychical Research.

According to the *Streatham News* of 9 September 1955, three psychical researchers (two men and a woman) duly visited her flat in early September. One of the men sat in a chair close to where Evelyn had seen the apparition, and put himself into a trance. Afterwards, he told Evelyn that she need not be afraid because the nun was not an evil spirit. This was good news, but unfortunately it came with a negative side: because the nun was not an evil spirit the psychical researchers were unable to carry out an exorcism.

'I am trying to get used to it,' Evelyn told the *Streatham News*. 'I just don't want people to think I am daft, that is all.'

Another tenant who claimed encounters with the phantom nun was a forty-year-old engineering inspector named in the *Streatham News* of 9 September 1955 as Frank Cunnington, although Peter Underwood, in his 1973 book *Haunted London*, gave the surname of what was presumably the same gentleman as Cunningham.

According to Underwood, Frank, who lived on a different floor to Evelyn Sayers, awoke one night to see the figure of a nun wearing a white habit. The nun stroked his brow, and he heard a voice say: 'God bless you, my son.' Whether he went back to sleep after this or the nun vanished is not stated.

Two nights later, Frank reportedly saw two white-robed nuns bending over his children's beds as they slept.

Underwood speculated that the apparitions seen in Coventry Hall might be 'a remnant of concentrated thought that lingered on in the building after it was altered for secular use.'

The old Coventry Hall in Streatham was reputedly haunted by the apparition of a nun. (© Anthony Wallis: www.ant-wallis-illustration.blogspot.co.uk.)

Not every resident supported the idea that Coventry Hall was haunted. One tenant, who did not want to be named publicly, wrote to the council to complain about the stories of apparitions. Children, he protested, were being frightened by the tales.

Evelyn Sayers disagreed, telling reporters: 'It is nonsense to say the children are frightened. On the contrary, they are putting blue mackintoshes around their heads and playing at being nuns. To them it is just a game.'

As interested parties searched for an explanation for the apparent haunting, attention was drawn to a report that human bones had previously been found on the site of Coventry Hall, a revelation that was reported to the *Streatham News* by Mrs Ethel Bromhead, vice-chairman of Streatham Historical Society.

Shortly before the Second World War, Mrs Bromhead and her late husband – an expert on Streatham's history – had been told by Coventry Hall's Mother Superior that the nuns had discovered human bones while digging in their kitchen garden. The Mother Superior had suggested that they were the bones of some of the monks who had been sent here from Chertsey in the seventh century by Wulfere, the Christian king of Mercia.

Musing on the idea that monks would have had a hallowed area for burying their dead, Mrs Bromhead wondered: 'Can it be possible that the recent breaking up by bulldozers [during the demolition work before the flats were built] of this ancient and holy bit of old Streatham is indirectly responsible for wandering souls seeking what they cannot find? These mysteries are too deep for the ordinary human mind to comprehend.'

In around the middle of September 1955, two further Coventry Hall tenants came forward to say that they, too, had had numerous encounters with the phantom nun in their flat over the previous eight years. This would date their first sighting back to around the time the flats first became available.

These tenants were two housewives: thirty-four-year-old Mrs Dorothy Savage and her sister-in-law, thirty-nine-year-old Mrs Lola Cooke, who shared a three-bedroom flat on the first floor in what the *Streatham News* (16 September) called 'the oldest part of the building, overlooking the main entrance'.

Dorothy described their ghostly lodger: 'She has never spoken to us or shown her face. All we see is the silhouetted figure in black robes. She appears to be solid, but if anyone speaks she vanishes. Sometimes we hear the swish of her gown as she passes.'

'She does not frighten us,' added Lola. 'She is a good spirit. We regard her as almost a friend.'

Dorothy went on to say: 'We see her in daylight and in the evening on an average of twice a week. Nearly always she walks about 30ft from the living room through the corridor in the bathroom. Then she disappears.'

Both women claimed that their husbands had also seen the nun, although each man had seen her on only one occasion.

Dorothy – referring to her husband, Arthur, a thirty-seven-year-old toolmaker – stated:

My husband pooh-poohs any talk about the other world, but last year, when I came back from holiday, he told me, 'I have seen your lady.' ...

He was washing up and looked up to see the nun in the hall. She walked into a bedroom. My husband was so certain it was a human being that he followed her. But the room was empty.

With reference to her own husband, an engineer in his fifties, Lola said: 'Victor is dead against anything like that, but he did admit that he saw her once.'

According to the two women, the apparition always emerged from their living room, which the newspaper described as 'a high-ceilinged corner room containing an Adam fireplace.'

'Sometimes my sister-in-law and I are together when we see her,' said Dorothy:

... [and] sometimes on our own. The nun is always accompanied by an atmosphere. No matter what you may be doing something compels you to look up. And that is when we see her. Once, I was sitting in broad daylight with a friend on the lawn. I glanced up and saw the black shape standing by my French windows. I turned away and then looked again. The nun was still there. But my friend could see nothing.

Although other tenants reportedly saw the ghost at night, Dorothy and Lola were clear that 'their' nun made her appearances during the day or evening. Given that they described the apparition they saw as wearing black robes – whereas Underwood reported that Frank Cunningham (or Cunnington) had seen nuns wearing white robes – perhaps the building had more than one phantom wandering around inside.

Fortunately for the sisters-in-law, neither Dorothy nor Lola found the haunting in the least bit frightening. To them, the most disagreeable aspect of their situation was that some doubted their story.

'The trouble is that you can't make people believe you,' said Dorothy, 'but I assure you we are far from being potty.'

There were indeed sceptics who doubted the ghost reports, with some suspecting an ulterior motive. Might it be, they wondered, that certain tenants were making up stories because they wanted to be moved to better council accommodation? As it happens, there was at this same time widespread resentment at the condition of Coventry Hall's flats.

That September, tenants had drawn up a list of complaints, demanding that they be re-housed, a demand the council rejected a few weeks later.

In mid-October, Mr Maurice Styles, the tenants' association secretary, told the *Streatham News*: 'I would like to pull this place down. It should never have been converted or requisitioned. It was a waste of public money.'

Another (unnamed) tenant was quoted as saying: 'I think it's disgusting. We have to pay £3 10s 6d for a flat in bad condition,' while yet others had apparently complained of damp and of 'crawly things' that infested the flats.

The sceptics' insinuations infuriated those who claimed Coventry Hall was haunted. Evelyn Sayers vehemently denied that the ghost reports were in any way connected with discontent at the state of the building. Back at the beginning of September, she announced:

I hear that some malicious people are saying I invented the story to force the council to re-house me. I will only point out two things to them. If I wanted to play a trick on the council I could have done it five years ago. Secondly, I am not the only one who has seen a nun. And there are others in the flats who can sense the peculiar atmosphere here.

Likewise, Dorothy Savage had said in mid-September: '... there are others who say tenants of Coventry Hall are seeing ghosts to wangle themselves a new council flat. Well, you can tell everyone that Mrs Cooke and I are quite all right where we are, thank you very much!'

According to a newspaper article that appeared in December 1957, a Roman Catholic priest was at some point called in to say prayers in Evelyn Sayers's flat, and to ask the ghostly nun to leave the residents of Coventry Hall in peace. Whether or not that helped was not made clear, the article merely stating diplomatically that 'Mrs Sayers later

moved from "Coventry Hall" – and for the past eighteen months the town hall has received no further ghostly complaints from its tenants.'

A few years later, the writer Dennis Bardens reported in his 1965 book *Ghosts & Hauntings* that all had been peaceful at Coventry Hall for 'the last few years'.

But the ghost stories were not over yet. To use the description from her own website, Dolly Sen is 'a writer, director, artist, film-maker, poet, performer, raconteur, playwright, mental-health consultant, music-maker and public speaker' who was born in October 1970. When she was very young, her family moved into one of the flats in Coventry Hall. In her 2002 book, *The World is Full of Laughter*, Dolly recalls an incident that occurred in either 1972 or 1973, when she was around two years old:

Our new home ... had quite a history and a lot of character. It was part of a large building which used to be a

In 1982 the old convent building was demolished. A new building, also named Coventry Hall, was built on the site.

convent. […] There was supposed to be a ghostly nun haunting the building. Most of the adults didn't see it and those that did were sent to the local Tooting Bec insane asylum. Almost all the kids saw it, including me, although I don't remember it. My Mum saw me talking to an empty space. 'Who are you talking to?' she asked. 'Nun. Nun,' I replied.

In 2011 I asked Dolly whether she could remember any further information about this. She responded:

I asked my mum about me seeing something. Not only did I point to something they couldn't see and say 'Nun', [but also] I was lifting my arms up as if to be lifted by the nun, and said, 'Pick me up'. I still don't remember it – which is a shame.

Dolly also passed along another story that her mother had told her about the ghost:

My dad came home with a friend after a gig – they were musicians. My dad was carrying some of his instruments up the stairs, thinking his friend was right behind him, but as he reached his front door his friend was nowhere to be seen. My dad called for him but he was gone. My dad thought his friend was just being lazy, and impolite for not saying goodnight. Anyway, the next day my dad phoned his friend and asked him where he went. Apparently, his friend was just about to climb the main stairs when he saw a nun at the top of the stairs just disappear. His friend didn't come back after that.

The old convent building was demolished in 1982, and today a different building stands on the site. Erected in 1995, this was specially designed to provide sheltered accommodation for the elderly. Although this new building has also been given the name Coventry Hall, to the best of my knowledge it has not inherited the former building's ghostly resident(s).

MAIN SOURCES

The Margate Road Horror

Clare, John, 'Psychic housing officer helps a haunted family', *News of the World*, 16 December 1979, p.11

Hutchinson, Diana, 'The haunted council house', *Daily Mail*, 21 December 1979, p.11

'Supernormal' Disturbances at The Gresham Arms

Atwood, Thomas, 'The Alleged Hauntings at Brixton', *Light* 21:1044, 12 January 1901, pp. 16–17

Goss, Michael, *Poltergeists: An Annotated Bibliography of Works in English, circa 1880-1975* (The Scarecrow Press, Inc., Metuchen, N.J. & London, 1979)

'W.C.L., 'The Brixton Haunting', *Light* 20:1028 (September 22, 1900), p. 452

The House that Haunted Roy Hudd

Hudd, Roy, personal communication, October 2011

Hudd, Roy, 'The house that haunted me', in *The Unexplained*, Issue 6 (Orbis Publishing Ltd, London, 1980)

The Devil in Disguise?

'I'm All Shook Up!', *South London Press*, 4 March 1994, pp.1, 2

'Spookbusters!', *South London Press*, 18 March 1994, p.18

Strange Tales from Clapham Common

'A Few Recollections of Clapham. The Common During the Past Sixty Years', *Clapham Observer*, 1 February 1924 (in Wandsworth Local History Service, *Wandsworth Notes*, vol. 6, p.93)

Bradbury, John, 'He fled into the past. A tale of the supernatural based on the true life story of Freddie Snucher', *South Western Star*, 27 August 1982, p.14

Bradbury, John, 'Trapped in a time bubble: Part Two', *South Western Star*, 10 September 1982, p.55

Bradbury, John, 'The twist at the end', *South Western Star*, 17 September 1982, p.53

O'Donnell, Elliot, *More Haunted Houses of London* (Eveleigh Nash Co. Ltd, London, 1920)

Worthington, Simon, 'Exit: 40 best places in the UK to be abducted by aliens', *The Sun*, 8 April 2004, p.43

The Spectral Hansom Cab of South Side

Bilbe, Harry Smith, personal account, *Evening News*, 6 February 1935 (in Wandsworth Local History Service, *Wandsworth Notes*, vol. 7, p.161)

The Haunting of the Plough Inn

'Pub staff seek a ghostly, murdered barmaid', *South London Press*, 18 September 1970, p.3

'The Vanishing Convict – and Other Ghostly Tales', *Wandsworth Borough News*, 23 December 1976, p.11

Bradbury, John, 'Phenomena of the third kind', *South Western Star*, 13 August 1982, p.47

Brooks, J.A., *Ghosts of London* (Jarrold Publishing, Norwich, 1991)

Green, Andrew, *Our Haunted Kingdom* (Wolfe Publishing Ltd, London, 1973)

McCormack, William (Manager, O'Neill's, 196 Clapham High Street), personal communication, July 2008

Playfair, Guy Lyon, *The Haunted Pub Guide* (Javelin Books, Poole, Dorset, 1987)

Thornbury, Walter, *Old and New London: A Narrative of its History, its People and its Places. Illustrated with Numerous Engravings from the Most Authentic Sources, Volume 6* (Cassell, Peter & Galpin, London, New York, 1872-78)

Underwood, Peter, *Haunted London* (Fontana, London, 1973)

The Black Dog of Wandsworth Road

Brooks, J.A., *Ghosts of London* (Jarrold Publishing, Norwich, 1991)

Ghost Stories of Lambeth Palace

Brooks, J.A., *Ghosts of London* (Jarrold Publishing, Norwich, 1991)

Bruce, Marie Louise, *Anne Boleyn* (Pan, 1972)

Clark, James, *Haunted London* (The History Press, Stroud, 2007)

Norton, Elizabeth (author of *Anne Boleyn: In Her Own Words & the Words of Those Who Knew Her*, www.elizabethnorton.co.uk), personal communication, February 2012

Nunn, Andrew (premises and administration secretary to the Archbishop of Canterbury), personal communication, April 2008

Pennant, Thomas, *Some Account of London* (5th edn, London, 1813)

Thornbury, Walter, *Old and New London: A Narrative of its History, its People and its Places. Illustrated with Numerous Engravings from the Most Authentic Sources, Volume 6* (Cassell, Peter & Galpin, London, New York, 1872-78)

Underwood, Peter, *Haunted London* (Fontana, London, 1973)

The Tomb of the Tradescants

Norman, Philip (volunteer curatorial assistant at the Museum of Garden History – now the Garden Museum), personal communication, April 2008

Mercy Weller's Ghost

Norman, Philip (volunteer curatorial assistant at the Museum of Garden History – now the Garden Museum), personal communication, April 2008

Osborn, Ann (head of the Junior

Department, Fairley House School), personal communication, April 2008

The Predatory Lift of Lincoln House

Beer, Lionel, personal communication, January 2009

Beer, Lionel, 'The Lift Man Cometh', *COIGN* (in-house magazine of the Central Office of Information), summer 1981

The Lingering Shadow of Waterloo's Necropolis Railway

Clarke, John M., personal communication, December 2011 – January 2012

Clarke, John M., *The Brookwood Necropolis Railway* (The Oakwood Press, Usk, 2006)

Geary, Rebecca (of Make Space Studios), personal communication, January 2012

Mann, Darren (of The Paranormal Database: www.paranormaldatabase.com), personal communication, November – December 2011

Railforums website, personal communication with following users at www.railforums.co.uk: 'Capybara', 'Clip', 'KiddyKid', 'SalopSparky', 'steamybrian', and 'thedbdiboy', January 2012

Ghosts at The Old Vic

Lewis, Roy Harley, *Theatre Ghosts* (David & Charles, London, 1988)

Seago, Ned (stage-door manager, The Old Vic theatre), personal communication, June 2008

Underwood, Peter, *Haunted London* (Fontana, London, 1973)

The Ghost of Norwood

'Crowds wait to see Ghost', *News Chronicle*, 17 July 1951, p. 3

'Exorcism attempt at West Norwood', *Two Worlds* 64:3324, 11 August 1951, p. 371

'"Ghost" House Family Has Had Enough', *South London Press*, 20 July 1951, p. 1

'"Ghost" was heard but not seen', *Norwood News*, 3 August 1951, p. 1

'House where family dare not go to bed', *News Chronicle*, 16 July 1951, p. 3

'Investigators puzzled by London case', *Two Worlds* 64:3323, 4 August 1951, p. 355

'Norwood ghost came back for bank holiday', *Norwood News*, 10 August 1951

'Norwood Ghost Comes Back', *Two Worlds* 64:3326, 25 August 1951, p. 391

'Norwood ghost has been laid', *Norwood News*, 27 July 1951, p. 1

'Police investigate "haunted house"', *Norwood News*, 20 July 1951, p. 1

'Poltergeist Still Active in Norwood', *South London Press*, 17 July 1951, p. 1

'Seven people leave home to a ghost', *Daily Express*, 18 July 1951, p. 1

'The Ghost Gone West?', *South London Press*, 24 July 1951, p. 1

Spencer, John and Anne, *The Encyclopedia of Ghosts and Spirits* (Headline, London, 1992)

Underwood, Peter, *Haunted London* (Fontana, London, 1973)

Tulse Hill Station and the Phantom Footsteps of Platform One

Hallam, Jack, *Ghosts of London* (Wolfe Publishing Ltd, London, 1975)

Herbert, W.B, *Railway Ghosts & Phantoms* (David & Charles, London, 1989)

Gipsy Hill: Fortune Tellers and a Headless Phantom

Allen, Thomas, *The History and Antiquities of the Parish of Lambeth, and the Archiepiscopal Palace, in the County of Surrey* (J. Allen, London, 1827)

Brandon, David and Brooke, Alan, *Haunted London Underground* (The History Press, Stroud, 2008)

Brooks, John, *The Good Ghost Guide* (Jarrold Publishing, Norwich, 1994)

The Stockwell Ghost

'Kennington and Stockwell in the 18th Century' (newspaper cutting, source unknown, retrieved from http://www.londonancestor.com/misc/bermondsey-stockwell.htm on 13 January 2012)

Golding, Mary; Pain, John; Pain, Mary; Fowler, Richard; Fowler, Sarah and Martin, Mary, *An authentic, candid, and circumstantial narrative of the astonishing transactions at Stockwell, in the county of Surrey, on Monday and Tuesday, the 6th and 7th days of January, 1772, containing a series of the most surprising and unaccountable events that ever happened; which continued from first to last upwards of twenty hours, and at different places* (London, 1772)

Lysons, Revd Daniel, *The Environs of London: Being an Historical Account of the Towns, Villages, and Hamlets, Within Twelve Miles of that Capital* (London, 1792-96)

Mackay, Charles, *Extraordinary Popular Delusions and the Madness of Crowds* (Three Rivers Press, New York, 1980; originally published in 1841 as *Memoirs of Extraordinary Popular Delusions*)

A Ghost on the Northern Line

Ghosts on the Underground (TV documentary, a Polar Media production for Five, Channel 5 Broadcasting Ltd, 2005)

The Many Ghosts of Caesars Nightclub

'Caesars Nightclub, South London', *Most Haunted*, series 2, vol. 2, Living TV, 2003

Batt, Fred, website (www.fredbatt.com) – accessed December 2011

Ellis, Georgie, with Taylor, Rod, *Ruth Ellis, My Mother: A Daughter's Memoir of the Last Woman to be Hanged* (Smith Gryphon Publishers, London, 1995)

Watts, Matt, 'Ghostbusters to inspect doomed Caesar's nightclub', 26 January 2009: http://www.streathamguardian.co.uk/news/4075421.Ghostbusters_to_inspect_doomed_nightclub/

Watts, Matt, 'Ghostbusters find "unexplained things" at "haunted" Caesers [sic] nightclub, 17 February 2009: http://www.thisislocallondon.co.uk/news/weird/4132227._Unexplained_things__found_at__haunted__club/

The Haunted House of Shrubbery Road

Pasha, Sofi, 'The House of Horrors', *South Western Star*, 9 March 1984, p. 43

The Phantom of the Cinema

'Hooded "Ghost" in a Cinema', *Daily Mail*, 28 December 1933 (in Lambeth Archives, Scrapbook No 1 (H W Bromhead) IV/66/6/11)

Brown, John W., 'Local Historian John W. Brown goes Christmas ghost hunting in Streatham', *Streatham, Clapham & Dulwich Guardian*, 19 December 2002, p. 4

Mortimer, Sussannah (cinema manager, Odeon Streatham), personal communication, November 2011

A Mysterious Light in Tankerville Road

'John' (pseudonym), personal communication, July 1998

The Phantom Nun of Coventry Hall

'Coventry Hall – latest revelation: A "friendly ghost" has lived there for eight years', *The Streatham News*, 16 September 1955 (in Lambeth Archives, cuttings made by Ethel Bromhead, IV/66/6/21 1949-56)

'Council meets Coventry Hall tenants', *The Streatham News*, 14 October 1955 (in Lambeth Archives, cuttings made by Ethel Bromhead, IV/66/6/21 1949-56)

'Human bones have been found there', *The Streatham News*, 9 September 1955, p. 1 (in Lambeth Archives, cuttings made by Ethel Bromhead, IV/66/6/21 1949-56)

'Tenants divided over ghost reports', *The Streatham News*, 9 September 1955, p. 1 (in Lambeth Archives, cuttings made by Ethel Bromhead, IV/66/6/21 1949-56)

Bardens, Dennis, *Ghosts & Hauntings* (The Zeus Press, London, 1965)

Sen, Dolly, personal communication, October 2011

Sen, Dolly, *The World is Full of Laughter* (Chipmunkapublishing, Essex, 2002)

Thomas, Leslie, 'The Nun Called By Night', *Evening News* (date unclear), December 1957 (in Lambeth Archives, cuttings made by Ethel Bromhead, IV/66/6/23, 1956-62)

Underwood, Peter, *Haunted London* (Fontana, London, 1973)

If you enjoyed this book, you may also be interested in...

Haunted London

JAMES CLARK

From heart-stopping accounts of apparitions, manifestations and related supernatural phenomena to first-hand encounters with ghouls and spirits, this collection of stories contains new and well-known spooky tales from famous sights and buildings in the centre of London. Drawing on historical and contemporary sources *Haunted London* contains a chilling range of ghostly phenomena. The colourful tales featured here create a scary selection of ghostly goings-on that is bound to captivate anyone interested in the supernatural history of the area.

978 0 7524 4459 8

Haunted Wandsworth

JAMES CLARK

From heart-stopping accounts of apparitions, manifestations and related supernatural phenomena to first-hand encounters with French poltergeists and prison spectres, this collection of stories contains both well-known and hitherto unpublished tales of the ghosts, mysteries and legends of Batersea, Balham, Putney, Tooting and Wandsworth. From the spectral son of Marie Antoinette to a haunting at the Battersea Dogs and Cats home, this scary selection of ghostly goings-on is bound to captivate anyone interested in the supernatural history of the area.

978 0 7524 4070 5

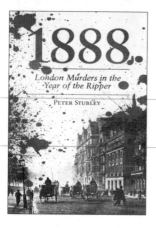

1888: London Murders in the Year of the Ripper

PETER STUBLEY

In 1888 Jack the Ripper made the headlines with a series of horrific murders that remain unsolved. But most killers are not shadowy figures stalking the streets. Many are ordinary citizens driven to the ultimate crime by circumstance, a fit of anger or a desire for revenge. Their crimes, overshadowed by the few sensational cases, are ignored, or forgotten. This book examines all the known murders in London in 1888 to build a picture of society. Who were the victims? How did they live, and how did they die?

978 0 7524 6543 2

Visit our website and discover thousands of other History Press books.

www.thehistorypress.co.uk